the
asian
collection

hamlyn

Editors: Sarah Ford and Anne Crane
Indexer: Hilary Bird

Executive Art Editor: Geoff Borin
Photographer: David Loftus
Food Stylist: Oona van den Berg
Stylist: Liz Hippisley

Production Controller: Joanna Walker

First published in 1999 by Hamlyn a division
of Octopus Publishing Group Ltd
2–4 Heron Quays
London E14 4JP

This paperback edition published in 2001

Copyright © 1999, 2001 Octopus Publishing Group Ltd

A CIP catalogue record for this book is available from the
British Library

ISBN 0 600 60392 X

Printed and bound in China

10 9 8 7 6 5 4 3 2 1

Notes:

Both imperial and metric measurements have been given in all
recipes. Use one set of measurements only and not a mixture of
both.

Standard level spoon measurements are used in all recipes.
1 tablespoon = one 15 ml spoon
1 teaspoon = one 5 ml spoon

Eggs should be large unless otherwise stated.

Milk should be full-fat unless otherwise stated.

Pepper should be freshly ground black pepper unless otherwise
stated.

Fresh herbs should be used unless otherwise stated. If unavailable,
use dried herbs as an alternative, but halve the quantities stated.

Nuts and nut derivatives.
This book includes dishes made with nuts and nut derivatives. It is
advisable for readers with known allergic reactions to nuts and nut
derivatives and those who may be potentially vulnerable to these
allergies, such as pregnant and nursing mothers, invalids, the elderly,
babies and children, to avoid dishes made with nuts and nut oils. It
is also prudent to check the labels of pre-prepared ingredients for
the possible inclusion of nut derivatives.

Ovens should be preheated to the specified temperature – if using
a fan-assisted oven, follow the manufacturer's instructions for
adjusting the time and the temperature.

Oona van den Berg

photography by David Loftus

traditional flavours from the east

contents

introduction

From Manila to Madras, Bombay to Bangkok, the cuisines of Asia are a subject as vast as the continent itself. The recipes in this collection come from all over south and east Asia, from India, Sri Lanka, Burma, China, Korea, Japan, Vietnam, Laos, Thailand, Cambodia, Malaysia and Singapore, the Philippines and Indonesia.

In the same way that Asia is a vast melting pot of cultures and religions, its cuisines are also a hybrid of disparate influences – the Moghuls in India, the French and Chinese in Vietnam, the Portuguese in Goa, Daman and Timor, the British in India, Malaysia and Burma, the Dutch in Indonesia and the Spanish in the Philippines. Each of these ruling powers brought with them new ingredients and ways of life and, to a greater or lesser extent, they have left their mark, most notably in the dishes they influenced, or left behind.

In the 16th century this part of Asia became a vital point in world trade, both for its natural wealth – timber, gems, gold and spices – and also because of its position on the global map. Places such as Singapore, Malacca, Cochin, Bangkok and Hoi An became important ports of call on the trade routes and merchants from all over the world arrived, bringing a host of influences.

Asian food is bright and colourful, with plenty of character supplied by the heat of red and green chillies, aromatic herbs and dry and fresh spices. Vegetables and fruits vary from country to country, from the Laotian wing beans to the bitter-tasting Thai aubergines and the long, thin Indian drumstick, a vegetable rather like a courgette, and the evil-smelling durian, to name but a few. These more unusual examples are found in the markets beside the more ordinary lettuces, dried lentils, beans, carrots and cabbages. Fish and seafood are popular in places with a shoreline, and dried prawns, pomfret and anchovies, in particular, are transported to villages far from the sea or rivers and rehydrated. Travelling further into the interior, particularly into the jungle areas, vegetables and game are more predominant.

Eating in Asia really brings meaning to the enjoyment of living. The time taken to prepare Indian, Chinese, Japanese or Thai dishes can be lengthy, but often the cooking time is short. In Indonesia, Burma and other less developed countries, cooking supper can mean beginning right at the start of the food preparation line by harvesting the ingredients or grinding the flour. Even in some parts of these countries fast food does exist; it is found in their night markets where plastic bags of curry, *larb*, *rojak* or *som tam* are bought by working mothers to supplement their cooking.

In South-east Asia the night markets, which are held every evening, are where everybody comes to eat. Customers sit at a simple folding table, either beside a *khlong* (canal), in Bangkok, or in the shadow of a temple, like those at Phimai in north-east Thailand, or standing by the side of a *murtabak* stall in Kota Baru, the Malaysian town across the border from Thailand. In India few people buy prepared dishes from the streets; but will go to a restaurant or coffee shop for a *masala dosa* or *idlies* or eat at home. However, travelling by train in India brings a wealth of food vendors past your carriage, selling hot samosas, hard-boiled eggs and pakoras along with the *chai* (tea) man. In the more developed countries of Singapore, Korea and Japan eating food sold by street vendors is a sanitised affair in air-conditioned food malls. The dishes are just as authentic but the style of street life is different.

Even a quick roadside snack involves a myriad of spices, herbs and other delectable ingredients. In Yangon, Jogjakarta or Penang the multitude of street vendors and hawkers tempt even the most fastidious of passers-by with their food. Every street has a vendor or restaurant, ranging from places with simple formica-topped tables, to formal restaurants with starched linen tablecloths and rattan chairs. In fact, eating out in some way or other is an everyday occurrence. To go to a market, even in a remote village in the middle of the Sumatran jungle, will always involve stopping at a *pulit hitam* stall, or, in Laos, to a stall set up near the bus stand, and frequented by passengers before a long journey.

In Europe we only come across a very small range of Asian dishes and in some cases they are bastardised versions of the real thing. Indian restaurants are all too often Bangladeshi, Vietnamese ones are run by Chinese, and Thai food is toned down to suit western tastes. To tramp the streets of any of these Asian countries is to learn that food is very much a valued part of everyday life. It is available from roadside stalls and street corner markets; it is enjoyed at home, and is part of the celebrations at weddings and name days (birthdays) and part of the ceremony at funerals. Food is ritualistic and honoured. Depending on the occasion, season or who you are, certain dishes will be offered.

To cook and provide food for guests is the greatest honour. The most memorable meals are those shared at home – wherever home may be. Asian food welcomes and is for sharing. It is a way of honouring the visitor, the ancestors and the generations to come.

Thailand

Thai food is subtle and complex, hot and unique, and unlike that of its neighbours, except Laos, which was once part of the same country. In the north, curries, game and meat accompany sticky rice and chilli is used with care. China has had a huge influence on Thai cuisine, in particular around Bangkok, where most of the Chinese settled. Now a cosmopolitan capital city, all styles of Thai cooking are found in Bangkok, as well as Chinese stir-fry dishes. Along the Mekong river, the mighty catfish is a speciality. In the far south, Muslim influences can be seen and the coconut is widely used. Its creamy milk flavours curries along with the distinctive hot chilli. Seafood is abundant. In the far north and north-east, frogs, ant eggs and even cicadas are on offer in the markets and are surprisingly tasty.

India

From the north to the south of the subcontinent, the regional variations in cooking are very marked. In the far north the influence is predominantly Moghul, with plenty of nuts, cream, buttermilk and dried fruit. Parathas, naan bread, tandoori chicken and meat kebabs are baked in tandoor clay ovens. In the far south the food is lighter and more simply cooked. Many of the people are primarily vegetarian, but do eat fish. The coconut is very much in evidence here with coconut-based vegetable dishes, sambals and dishes fried in coconut oil. These dishes are redolent with the heat of the chilli and plenty of garlic. A variety of wet vegetable curries, coconut sambal, dal, lime pickle and rice are offered on a banana leaf thali; they are eaten with the fingers and washed down with pepper water. On the west coast, Goanese cooking was heavily influenced by the Portuguese; there they use tomatoes, garlic, plenty of chilli, sugar and vinegar. To the east the food is similar to that in Burma, and there is plenty of seafood. An Indian meal always consists of a curry, rice, a bread and vegetable. Pickles and a variety of sambals or raitas are served at every meal. Desserts which are very sweet are popular on feast days.

Sri Lanka
Formerly known as Ceylon, this island has been influenced by the Dutch, English, Malays and Portuguese. Intensely hot curries are regularly cooked. Plenty of dried chillies give a deep red colour to fish and seafood curries, otherwise aromatic blends of dry spices, toasted until dark, are used to create rich curry sauces. Coconut-based curries are peppered with red chilli, but are otherwise mild. Curries are always served with rice and a bread. Deep-fried puris, unleavened rotis flavoured with shredded fresh coconut and lacy, pancake-like, *appas* with a coconut sambal are often available at lunch or dinnertime. The meal is completed with a soup and vegetable dishes.

Burma
Burma is situated between India, Thailand and China, and foods from all these countries, such as lemon grass, coriander, coconuts, fish sauce and soy sauce, chickpeas and dried mushrooms, are found in Burmese recipes. With its long coastline, fish is an important feature; they are fried simply or added to rich curry sauces and aromatic soups. Strongly flavoured curries are the centrepiece of each meal, particularly in the north. Chilli hot balachaung is a popular condiment that is added to all dishes. Burmese food is traditionally eaten with fingers.

Indonesia
This huge archipelago, which consists of more than 17,000 islands, was colonised by the Dutch in the 17th century, but all that lingers from those days is the *rijsttafel* (rice table), the Dutch name for a large buffet of Indonesian-style dishes. Overall the strongest culinary influences came from Arabia and India, and a strong Indian influence is still evident in Bali and Lombok. Central Java is where most of the rice is grown and where the majority of rice dishes originate. Further south the use of chillies becomes more marked. In the south-west, in the Moluccas, seafood and spices such as cloves, nutmeg and mace are widely used.

Malaysia & Singapore
Colonised by the English and Dutch, and with dishes originating from Arabia, Thailand and the Straits Chinese, this is a highly cosmopolitan region. Singapore, in particular, is a good place to experience a cross-section of South-east Asian cuisine, for the Indian, Arab and Chinese communities have kept themselves separate. Their traditions are strong and very much alive. Malacca is famed for Nonya cooking, a rich combination of Malay and Chinese ingredients and styles, which have merged to create a new and distinctive type of cooking.

China
This is the oldest cuisine in the world. An everyday meal includes rice, wheat buns or noodles with braised, roasted or stir-fried dishes and a soup. Traditionally the food is eaten from small china bowls with blunt-ended chopsticks and accompanied by small cups of green or jasmine tea, or, on special occasions, rice wine.

There are four regional styles. In the north, bread, pancakes and noodles are eaten as much as rice. Lamb is more common than pork,

and roasting is popular but very little spice or chilli are used. On the east coast there are rich braised dishes and stewing is popular. Thick, meaty dishes are served with noodles and there are freshwater and sea fish. In the central and western areas the dishes are vibrant, colourful and packed with flavour. Chilli is much used, as are garlic, ginger and fermented black beans. In the south, where the dishes are more subtle, pork, chicken, shrimp and fish are steamed and stir-fried.

Japan
Japanese cooking is artistry itself and adheres to strict rituals. The key is simplicity, ingredients of the highest quality and a painstakingly achieved visual display. Freshness is vital. Japan has few regional differences in cooking or ingredients. Except at a banquet, which will consist of many courses, all the dishes arrive at once. They are eaten with pointed chopsticks, and accompanied by thick soy sauce, wasabi, or finely grated daikon. There is green tea to drink or warm sake.

Korea
Korean food is of high quality and served simply. Fish and meat dishes are marinaded and served with dips and dressings and kimchi, the powerful national pickle. Many dishes are cooked at the table on a Mongolian barbecue stone or in a steamboat warmed by burning coals.

Phillipines
The mainstays of the diet here are rice and fish. The Spanish colonisers introduced tomatoes, garlic, olive oil and vinegar and there are also Malay and Chinese elements in the cooking. More recently, there has been a considerable American influence.

Laos
The food here is similar to that of north-east Thailand. The Laotians eat plenty of sticky rice but, being a landlocked, jungle-covered country, meat is kept for special occasions. Cucumbers, tomatoes, winged beans and water spinach are grown and vegetarian dishes and freshwater fish are eaten most days. Surprisingly, in this part of Asia, dry spices are not used, since the trade never reached here. Although part of the French Indo-Chinese empire, Laos was mostly left untouched.

Cambodia
Cambodia's culinary history has been strongly influenced by its neighbours Vietnam and Thailand and by the Mons, the early conquerors from India. Later it was colonised by the French, who introduced classic French dishes and ingredients. Fish features predominately in the diet and there are aromatic steamboats of fish and seafood. Coriander and mint are eaten at virtually every meal and the sour tang of the tamarind is often present. Meat is grilled in the form of satay or cooked in aromatic curries, spiked with chilli.

Vietnam
The Vietnamese have an elegant but simple way of cooking. It is similar to the Chinese style but uses less oil, more herbs and vegetables and is highly aromatic. Chinese medicinal herbs and roots are often used, and so are tofu and noodles. The chilli is not so popular as in Thailand but fragrant basil, lemon grass, lime leaves and fish sauce are used a lot. Fresh herbs accompany most meat dishes and are used in fragrant broths which are eaten everyday. Legacies of the French past are in evidence, with baguettes, frogs' legs and pâtés on most menus.

glossary

This glossary contains brief descriptions of some of the more unusual ingredients used in this book. They are available from Chinese, Indian or Asian stores or supermarkets.

Balachaung
A hot Burmese condiment made from deep-fried shallots, garlic, chillies and dried shrimps. Available in jars, it accompanies most Burmese meals.

Bamboo
These succulent shoots are used extensively in Asian cooking. Use canned or fresh.

Banana
This plant supplies Asia with a multitude of products, from the fruit, which ranges from large green bananas, more like plantains, which are added to pickles or served as a vegetable accompaniment, to the tiny sweet apple bananas which are used in puddings. The banana flower is boiled or steamed and added to salads or used as a crudité with dips. The banana leaf is made into bowls with the aid of a cocktail stick or laid flat to serve as a plate. All types of bananas are available in Asian stores and the leaves can be found fresh and frozen. Thawed frozen leaves are ideal for wrapping fish for the barbecue, as they do not need to be blanched first.

Basil
Often used in Thai and Vietnamese cooking. Holy basil has a purple stem and purple/green leaves. It has an intense flavour when cooked. Sweet basil, generally larger than holy basil, has a stronger flavour and a more delicate green leaf. Both are different from Italian basil but if they are hard to find use the Mediterranean version.

Bean curd (tofu)
A firm or soft curd cake made from the soya bean and used as a source of protein in China, Japan and throughout South-east Asia. Available in Asian stores or supermarkets. Japanese tofu, known as cotton bean curd, is usually softer, whiter and more delicate than regular bean curd. Bean curd is kept in water to prevent it drying out and should be chilled until required. Fried bean curd is used in braised or stir-fried dishes for its texture as it retains its shape when cooked.

Black fungus (cloud ear fungus)
A dried crinkly black fungus, sometimes with a beige underside, often used in Chinese and Thai cooking. It is rehydrated by soaking in hot water for 10–15 minutes before use.

Bonito flakes
Dried, paper-thin flakes of tuna, vital for making Japanese dashi stock.

Catfish
A freshwater fish much used in Thai and Laotian cooking. It can be found frozen in Asian stores, otherwise use monkfish, sea bass or bream.

Chickpea flour
(chana dal powder, gram or besan)
Chickpeas and chickpea flour are Indian staples. The flour is used to make batters for pakoras, onion *bhajis* and some sweet dishes. Sold in health food stores and Asian shops.

Chillies
These are synonymous with Asian cooking. Red chillies are the hottest, and generally the smaller the chilli the hotter the effect. The Thais favour the tiny red bird chillies, which are like dynamite and should be used with caution. They also use the very mild cayenne or yellow chillies. If you deseed chillies their effect will be milder. In this book, unless stated, the seeds have been left in. Your choice. Dried chillies give a more mellow flavour, but also vary in strength. Large, mildly flavoured Kashmiri chillies are now available in supermarkets. Dried Japanese (*togarashi*) chillies are the hottest.

Chinese dates (jujubes)
These small, dried, bright red dates are found in oriental shops. Used in braised Chinese dishes, they need to be soaked in boiling water for at least 2 hours, or preferably overnight.

Chinese rice wine
Aromatic red and white wines are made from fermented rice and millet. Use French vermouth as a substitute. Shaoxing rice wine is a rich amber colour and used extensively in cooking. Found in Asian stores.

Coconut
The flesh, juice and milk of the coconut are essential to southern Indian, Sri Lankan, Thai, Malaysian and Indonesian cooking. Coconut milk is added to curries for its rich flavour and creamy texture. Use blocks of creamed coconut, dissolved first in boiling water, or cans of coconut milk. In Asia coconut milk is made from the grated flesh of the coconut with water. However, cans of coconut milk are quicker and easier. Desiccated coconut can be used for its concentrated flavour and texture. Coconut water, the clear liquid from the centre of a fresh coconut, is used as a stock for soups. It is sold in ring-pull cans in Asian stores.

Coriander
A vital ingredient. The leaves are used extensively for their flavour and as a garnish. The stalk and root are also used in Thai curry pastes. Keep in the refrigerator in a paper bag.

Curry leaves
Used in Indian and South-east Asian cooking. The leaves have a warm aroma and delicate spicy taste. Add whole or ground to curries, pickles and fish dishes.

Curry pastes
A variety of ready-made curry pastes are available in supermarkets and Asian stores. Indian and Thai pastes can be made at home. Thai curry pastes depend on a mix of spices, garlic, chillies, lemon grass, herbs and a shallot. Chilli-hot green Musaman (see page 69), yellow and red are the most popular Thai curries. The pastes can be kept in the refrigerator in an airtight jar for 2–3 weeks. To make a red curry paste blend together 10 fresh red chillies, 2 teaspoons coriander seeds, 5 cm (2 inch) piece of galangal, 1 stalk lemon grass, 4 garlic cloves, 1 shallot, ½ teaspoon shrimp paste and 1 teaspoon lemon juice.

Daikon (mooli)
A large tapered white radish with a slightly hot flavour, grated and served as a condiment with Japanese food.

Dashi
A stock (see page 17) made from kombu seaweed and bonito flakes and used extensively in Japanese cooking.

Deep-fried shallots
Used in South-east Asia as a garnish and sold ready-fried in Asian stores. To cook from fresh, finely slice shallots and deep-fry in hot oil until crisp and golden brown. Drain well on kitchen paper. Garlic can be cooked in the same way.

Dried anchovies (ikan bilis)
Dried fish is used extensively in Asian countries where fresh fish are at a premium or unavailable. Wash off the excess salt in plenty of cold water.

Dried shrimp
Used in Thai cooking to flavour fried noodles and in salads. They vary in size from tiny to the medium sized prawns. Rinse thoroughly, cover with boiling water and leave to stand for 30 minutes before using. Keep dried shrimp in an airtight container or double wrap and store in the freezer.

Fenugreek (methi)
The oval seeds are used throughout Asia but the green leaves (*methi*) are used in cooking only in India and Burma. Sold in Indian stores. Use young spinach as a substitute for fresh fenugreek.

Fermented black beans
Used in Chinese braised dishes and stir-fried dishes, these beans are sold in cans and vacuum packs. They are also used to make black bean paste.

Fish sauce
This very salty sauce made from fermented fish is a vital ingredient in Thai, Vietnamese, Laotian, Cambodian and Malaysian cooking.

Five spice powder
A mix of star anise, cassia bark, Sichuan pepper, fennel and cloves. Used liberally in Chinese cooking.

Flowering chives (gau choy fa)
These long chives have pointed flower heads. Use raw as a garnish or stir-fry as a vegetable. Keep in damp paper at the bottom of the refrigerator.

Galangal
Similar to root ginger but more pungent. If galangal is not available use twice the quantity of root ginger. Sold in Asian stores.

Ghee
This is the traditional cooking fat of India and made from clarified butter or, in the case of vegetable ghee, from pure vegetable oils. It can be heated to high temperatures.

Ginger
Used throughout Asia for its hot, aromatic flavour. Choose firm tubers and keep chilled until required. To make 1 tablespoon of ginger juice, put 3 tablespoons of roughly chopped ginger in a garlic crusher and squeeze through.

Gingko nuts
Small cream-coloured nuts added to simmered dishes, desserts and soups. Cashew nuts can be substituted.

Ground fish (Maldive fish)
A dried fish powder used in Chinese and Burmese dishes. Available in cans from Asian shops.

Ground roasted rice
Used in Thai cooking. Roast in the oven or in a hot, dry frying pan until golden brown. Cool before grinding coarsely. Keep in an airtight container.

Kaffir lime
Both the fruit and the leaves are used for their aromatic qualities. The glossy, oval leaves are used in much the same way as bay leaves and add a delicious sharp citrus taste. Buy fresh from Asian stores or freeze-dried from the spice section of the supermarket.

Kimchi
A Korean pickle with a strong kick made from Chinese cabbage, fish sauce, onions, garlic, ginger and chilli powder. Served at every Korean meal.

Lemon grass
Long tapering stalks used in South-east Asian curries, soups and curry pastes. Peel away the outer leaves and bruise a piece of stalk with the handle of a knife or chop finely.

Mango
One of the most popular fruits in Asia, green mangoes are used in savoury dishes, ripe ones in desserts.

Mint
An important ingredient in Indian, Thai, Cambodian, Vietnamese and Laotian cooking. Asian mints vary but European mint can be used instead.

Mirin
A sweet yellow Japanese wine used only for cooking. Found in Asian stores and some large supermarkets.

Miso
These fermented soya pastes are a vital Japanese ingredient. Generally speaking, the lighter the miso, the milder the flavour and greater the sweetness. Available in health food and Asian stores.

Mushrooms
Enoki are Japanese mushrooms with long thin stems and small creamy yellow caps. Available in some supermarkets. Shiitake are brown-capped mushrooms available fresh or dried. They are used in Chinese and

Japanese cooking. Straw mushrooms which look like tiny eggs are available in cans. Oyster mushrooms are used in Chinese and Japanese cooking for their delicate colour and subtle flavour. Available in supermarkets.

Noodles
Rice noodles range from thick, flat noodles to rice vermicelli (*mei fun*, *meehoon*, *sen mee*, *banh hoi*), very fine strands which are stir-fried, used in soups or deep-fried and added as a garnish to Chinese dishes. Bean thread vermicelli (cellophane noodles) are transparent noodles made from mung beans. They must be soaked in hot water or briefly boiled until just soft whereas rice vermicelli only need soaking in hot water before deep-frying or stir-frying. Vietnamese bun noodles are like spaghetti in size and shape and are used in soups. They are available fresh or dried. Egg noodles (*mie*) are used throughout Asia in soups and stir-fried dishes. They vary in shape and size and are available fresh or dried. They need to be rinsed, to remove the excess oil that coats them, before cooking. Wheat noodles (*somen*) can be round or flat and are usually sold dried. Udon noodles are a wheat noodle available fresh and dried. Buckwheat noodles (*soba*) are made from a mixture of buckwheat and wheat flours. They are boiled until softened and then refreshed under running cold water to prevent them overcooking and sticking together.

Pak choi/bok choy
This universal South-east Asian vegetable is available in supermarkets and Asian stores. There are many varieties and all can be interchanged.

Palm sugar (jaggery)
A dark brown, unrefined sugar used throughout Asia. Use soft dark brown muscovado sugar as a substitute.

Pandanus (rampe, screwpine)
This distinctive leaf is used in desserts for the vanilla-like flavour it gives to coconut milk. It is also used to wrap foods before they are cooked over coals. Found only in Asian stores.

Papaya (paw paw)
A large green-skinned fruit. Thai papaya is much larger than the orange fleshed varieties available in the supermarket and is used unripe for salads. Found in Asian stores.

Pea aubergine
Tiny pea-sized green aubergines, added at the end of cooking to Thai green curries.

Rice
The staple food of Asia. Long-grain basmati rice from India is considered one of the best quality rices. Thai fragrant rice is an aromatic slightly sticky long-grain rice. True sticky rice or glutinous rice has a high starch content. It is often steamed in banana leaves and is always eaten with the hands. Japanese rice (*haiga-mai*) has smaller oval grains and a high gluten content. Black rice (*pulit hitam*) is an Indonesian and Philippine speciality. It has a nutty flavour and is often used in puddings. Rice needs to be washed several times before cooking to remove the excess starch.

Rice paper (banh trang)
These come in rounds or triangles and are used as wrappers for spring rolls.

Roasted peanuts
Unsalted, skinned peanuts are roasted until golden brown, cooled and then crushed using a pestle and mortar. Keep in an airtight container.

Sambal ulek
An Indonesian red chilli sauce served as a condiment. Buy in bottles from Asian stores.

Seaweed
Used in Japanese cooking for its texture and high nutritional value. Packs of multi-coloured seaweeds are rehydrated and used for salads. Nori are sheets of dark seaweed rolled round sushi. Wakame is a fine curly seaweed added to soups and kombu is a dried seaweed used to flavour dashi. Available in oriental stores and some health food shops.

Seven spice pepper (shichimi)
A Japanese condiment made from dried chilli, Sichuan pepper, sesame seeds, nori, mandarin peel, hemp seeds and poppy seeds.

Shrimp paste (trasi, belcan)
A very concentrated shrimp or fish paste used a great deal in South-east Asian cooking. It gives dishes their authentic flavour and is much used in Thai curry pastes. Found in small jars in Asian stores.

Soy sauce
Shoyu is a dark Japanese soy sauce which is naturally fermented. *Tamari* is another Japanese soy sauce; it is dark and thick with an intense soy flavour. Other soy sauces include *Kekap manis*, Indonesian sweet soy sauce, which is dark, thick and aromatic. It is used extensively as a flavouring in Indonesian cooking and served

alongside satay. Light soy sauce is lighter in colour but saltier in flavour. It is used when a lighter colour is required when cooking.

Star anise
A star-shaped spice used in Vietnamese and Chinese cooking for its liquorice flavour.

Tamarind
A long brown pod with seeds and a tangy pulp used throughout Asian as a souring ingredient. It is available in pod form, as a compressed block and as a concentrated liquid. The blocks are the easiest to use and the best. To make tamarind water, pull off a 50 g (2 oz) piece, pour 300 ml (½ pint) of boiling water over it and leave for 20 minutes to soften. Strain to remove the seeds and stringy matter and use as requested in recipes. If tamarind is not available use lemon juice.

Tempe
A fermented soybean cake used in Malaysian and Indonesian cooking. Sold frozen in Asian stores. Plain or fried tofu can be used as a substitute.

Teriyaki
A Japanese meat or fish dish served with a sweet sauce made from sake, mirin, dark soy sauce and sugar. Make your own sauce or buy it ready-made from supermarkets.

Turmeric
A golden ground spice used throughout Asia for its colour particularly in Muslim and Indian cooking.

Vinegar
Distilled rice vinegar is used across Asia. It is used in sweet and sour dishes in India, China, Thailand, the Philippines, Japan and Vietnam.

Wasabi
A strong green Japanese horseradish condiment. Available as a powder or a paste. It is used to give a distinctive hot mustard taste to some sushi. Found in Asian stores.

Water spinach (ong choi)
This water vegetable grows near running water and has pointed leaves and a fat hollow stem. It is similar to watercress. Used in gado-gado and stir-fried as a vegetable.

Yard beans (long beans)
These beans are so named because they grow up to 1 yard (90 cm) long. Often seen in Asian stores curled into a coil. Prepare as normal beans and, if unavailable, use large western beans.

soups, starters & snacks

In most Asian countries all the dishes arrive together and so a soup will be served at the same time as the curry and rice. Likewise Thai Satay (see page 31) and Indian Pakoras (see page 26) are often considered a starter in the west but can form part of the main course. Soups are often a meal in themselves and are eaten for breakfast, lunch and dinner. In Hanoi, the capital of Vietnam, Pho Bo (see page 12) reigns supreme, in Thailand it is, Tom Kha Gai (see page 15) and in China, Wonton Soup (see page 16).

beef & flat noodle soup

pho bo, vietnam

Noodle soup is the classic soup of South-east Asia. It originates from China, but it is eaten in Thailand, where it is known as kuaytiaw nam, as a staple breakfast or mid-morning snack. It is most in evidence on the streets of Hanoi, the capital of Vietnam, where it is called pho bo and appears to be eaten on every street corner. The hawkers assemble the contents in a large china or melamine bowl right before your eyes. Breakfast, mid-morning snack, lunch in a hurry or last thing at night, pho bo *is just the thing. Even in Seattle, home of displaced Vietnamese,* pho bo *cafés are the places to find off-duty chefs eating. Serve with a Chinese soup spoon and chopsticks.*

1 Heat a large dry frying pan until very hot and sear the chuck steak or braising beef on all sides until brown and charred.

2 Place the beef in a large saucepan with the stock, star anise, cinnamon, black peppercorns, 1 sliced onion or 2 shallots, the garlic and ginger. Bring to the boil, removing any scum, and continue to boil for about 10 minutes. Reduce the heat, cover the pan with a lid and simmer for about 2 hours or until the beef is tender.

3 Blanch the bean sprouts in boiling water for 1 minute.

4 Cook the rice noodles in boiling water for 3–4 minutes or until just soft. Do not overcook them. Drain well and place in 4 large soup bowls. Arrange the bean sprouts, spring onions, coriander leaves, and the remaining onions or shallots over the noodles.

5 To make the *nuoc cham* sauce, pound the chopped chilli, garlic and sugar until smooth, using a pestle and mortar. Add the lime juice, vinegar, fish sauce and water and blend together well.

6 When the beef from the broth is tender, lift it out, slice it thinly and divide between the soup bowls with the slices of raw fillet and garnish with the red bird chillies.

7 Strain the broth, return it to the pan and season to taste with fish sauce, salt and pepper. To serve, ladle the hot broth over the contents of the bowls and serve immediately with the *nuoc cham* sauce and a plate of extra bean sprouts, spring onions, red chilli and lime wedges.

Serves 4–6

---

500 g (1 lb) chuck steak or a piece of braising beef

1.8 litres (3 pints) quality beef stock or water

4 star anise

1 large cinnamon stick

1 teaspoon black peppercorns

2 sweet onions or 4 shallots, thinly sliced

4 garlic cloves, crushed

7 cm (3 inch) piece of fresh root ginger, peeled and finely sliced

125 g (4 oz) bean sprouts

250 g (8 oz) dried flat rice noodles (*banh pho*)

6 spring onions, thinly sliced

handful of coriander leaves

250 g (8 oz) fillet of beef, thinly sliced

2 tablespoons fish sauce

salt and pepper

red bird chillies, to garnish

Nuoc cham sauce:

2 red chillies, chopped

1 garlic clove

1½ tablespoons caster sugar

1 tablespoon lime juice

1 tablespoon rice vinegar

3 tablespoons fish sauce

4 tablespoons water

To serve:

bean sprouts

thin spring onions, sliced

1 large red chilli, sliced

lime wedges

sour fish soup with lemon grass & mushrooms

keng som yum pa kho, laos

1 whole trout or whiting, weighing 750 g (1½ lb), scaled and gutted

1.2 litres (2 pints) water

1 garlic bulb

8 spring onions

3 lemon grass stalks

3 red bird chillies

4 coriander roots, finely chopped

75 g (3 oz) sour or unripe pineapple, rind and core removed

125 g (4 oz) shiitake or straw mushrooms, halved

2–3 tablespoons fish sauce

175 g (6 oz) pickled bamboo shoots (optional)

juice and finely chopped flesh of 2 limes

3 tablespoons chopped coriander leaves

1 tablespoon chopped holy basil leaves

To serve:

handful of coriander leaves, chopped

handful of holy basil leaves, chopped

2 large red chillies, sliced

Sour fish soup is traditionally made in Laos with snakehead fish, sometimes just with the head, tail and bones, which are discarded once the stock has been made. The characteristic sour flavour in this soup is created in two ways, either with a combination of lime juice and unripe pineapple, as here, or by adding tamarind. Both ways are delicious.

1 Fillet the fish. Cut the fillets into 5 cm (2 inch) slices and set aside. Place the head, tail and bones of the fish in a large saucepan with the water.

2 Peel and roughly chop 4 of the garlic cloves and 4 of the spring onions, slightly flatten 2 of the lemon grass stalks, and bruise the chillies with a rolling pin. Add to the saucepan with the coriander roots and bring to the boil. Reduce the heat and simmer for 25 minutes. Strain the stock and discard the fish head, tail and bones.

3 Chop the remaining lemon grass and garlic cloves, cut the pineapple into chunks and add them to the fish stock with the shiitake mushrooms. Simmer for 5 minutes to release the flavours.

4 Just before serving, add the reserved pieces of fish, chop the remaining spring onions and add with the fish sauce. Simmer gently for 5–6 minutes or until the fish has just cooked through.

5 Add the pickled bamboo shoots, if using, and the lime juice and flesh to the broth. Then add the chopped coriander and basil leaves and heat through. Serve ladled into large china bowls with extra herbs and the red chillies.

Serves 4

chicken, galangal & coconut soup

tom kha gai, thailand

500 g (1 lb) boneless, skinless chicken breasts

7 cm (3 inch) piece of galangal, peeled and thinly sliced

2 coriander roots, finely chopped (optional)

1 lemon grass stalk, finely sliced

3 kaffir lime leaves

400 ml (14 fl oz) coconut milk

150 ml (¼ pint) water

4 red bird chillies

2 teaspoons Burnt Chilli Paste (nam prik pow) (see page 81)

2 tablespoons lime juice

2 tablespoons fish sauce

steamed jasmine rice, to serve

handful of coriander leaves, to garnish

Like all soups in Thailand, this soup or 'wet' curry is eaten with freshly steamed jasmine rice. Fantastically quick and easy to make, soups (tom) are an integral part of the meal and are served alongside the fried dishes and salads. Burnt chilli paste can be bought from oriental stores, otherwise use the recipe on page 81.

1 Slice the chicken into thin strips and place them in a large saucepan or wok. Add the galangal, the coriander roots, if using, and the lemon grass.

2 Place the lime leaves one on top of each other, fold them in half and snip into fine shreds. Add to the chicken with the coconut milk and water and bring slowly to the boil.

3 Add the whole red chillies, the chilli paste, lime juice and fish sauce and stir well to combine the ingredients. Simmer gently for 5–6 minutes or until the chicken is cooked through. Serve in bowls with steamed jasmine rice, garnished with coriander leaves.

Serves 4

egg & beansprout moon soup

sup rau, vietnam

250 g (8 oz) thick, dried egg noodles (*ramen*)

900 ml (1½ pints) chicken stock

1½ tablespoons soy sauce

150 g (5 oz) bean sprouts

2 spring onions, sliced diagonally

4 eggs

salt and pepper

Moon-viewing noodles is best known as a simple Japanese soup containing a raw egg which lightly cooks in the hot broth. This version of moon soup was cooked by a wizened old man, who, with his wife, runs a soup (pho) stall in Sapa market. Sapa sits in the shadow of Fansipan, a mountain in the far north of Vietnam, right on the border of China. The soup was divine – the chicken stock the best and the eggs really, really fresh.

1 Bring a pan of water to the boil and cook the dried noodles for 3–4 minutes or until just done. Drain well and divide between 4 soup bowls making a nest in the centre of each one.

2 Bring the stock to a fast simmer, add the soy sauce, and season with salt and pepper. Blanch the bean sprouts and sliced spring onions in boiling water for 1 minute. Pour the hot stock over the noodles and immediately crack an egg into the centre of each soup bowl. Top the soup with the blanched bean sprouts and spring onions, and serve with a soup spoon and chopsticks. Each diner mixes the egg into the soup just before eating to help it cook.

Serves 4

wonton soup

hundun tang, china

Wontons originated long ago in Beijing (Peking), in the north of China, where wheat and millet are eaten as much as rice. These stuffed parcels float in an amber stock and make a fine first course. Fresh wonton pastry is easily bought from Chinese supermarkets, ready cut into squares. Any extra, uncooked wontons, can be frozen, ready to add to soups.

1 First make the filling. Chop the fish and crabmeat very finely with the spring onions, ginger and garlic or place all the ingredients in a food processor and blend to a paste.

2 Place 1 teaspoon of the mixture on a wonton wrapper, brush around the filling with a little water and fold the wrapper over to make a triangle. Repeat with the remaining mixture until all the wontons are made. Keep the unused wrappers covered with a damp cloth to prevent them drying out before filling them.

3 Put the stock into a saucepan with the shallots or small onion and sliced ginger and bring to the boil. Reduce the heat and add the sugar and filled wontons. Simmer gently for 5 minutes.

4 Add the spring onions, soy sauce, vinegar, parsley, salt and pepper. Just before serving add the sesame oil. Serve in individual bowls with soup spoons accompanied by small dishes of chilli oil.

Serves 4

20 wonton wrappers

1.2 litres (2 pints) chicken stock

2 pink Asian shallots or 1 small onion, finely chopped

2.5 cm (1 inch) piece of fresh root ginger, peeled and finely sliced

1 teaspoon caster sugar

4 spring onions, finely sliced

½ tablespoon light soy sauce

1 teaspoon rice vinegar

handful of roughly chopped parsley

1 teaspoon sesame oil

salt and pepper

chilli oil, to serve

Filling:

125 g (4 oz) white fish or prawns

125 g (4 oz) white crabmeat

2 spring onions, finely chopped

2.5 cm (1 inch) piece of fresh root ginger, peeled and finely chopped

1 garlic clove, crushed

miso soup with tofu

miso-shiru, japan

Western ways have caught on in Japan but miso soup is still the starting point to the Japanese day and is eaten right through to the end. Basically miso comes in two types, the lighter white miso which is ideal for summertime and the heavier red miso, which is eaten in the autumn and winter. The secret of miso soup is never to allow it to boil or the living enzymes will die and the flavour will be altered.

1 First make the dashi. Wipe the kombu seaweed with a damp cloth and place it in a saucepan with the water. Bring to a simmer, skimming away any scum that rises to the surface. When the soup is clear, add 1½ tablespoons of the dried tuna flakes and simmer uncovered for 20 minutes. Remove the pan from the heat and add the remaining dried tuna flakes. Set aside for 5 minutes then strain the dashi and return to the pan.

2 Mix the miso with a little of the warm stock and add 1 tablespoon at a time to the stock, stirring all the time until the miso has dissolved. Remove from the heat until ready to serve.

3 Cut the leek into fine julienne strips and the tofu into small squares. Warm the miso soup and add the leek and tofu with the wakame seaweed.

4 Blanch the chives, tie into a bundle and float on top of the soup and sprinkle with sansho pepper. Serve immediately.

Serves 4

2 tablespoons red or white miso

1 small leek

125 g (4 oz) firm tofu

1 tablespoon wakame seaweed

Dashi stock:

15 g (½ oz) kombu seaweed

1.8 litres (3 pints) water

2 tablespoons dried tuna (*bonito*) flakes

To serve:

chives

sansho pepper

steamboat soup

samla mchon, cambodia

The mighty Mekong River flows through Cambodia, from China all the way to the Gulf of Thailand. The catch netted off its south coast keeps the Cambodian kitchen well supplied with freshwater fish and seafood. Inland and away from the river, dried fish and seafood, in particular dried prawns, squid and pomfret are frequently used. This cook-at-the-table steamboat is a popular way of poaching morsels of seafood in an aromatic stock of tart ingredients. Everyone digs in and serves themselves. If you don't have a steamboat then a large saucepan is a good alternative.

1 Heat the vegetable oil in a small pan and when it is hot deep-fry the garlic, a few slices at a time, until golden brown. Remove the garlic and drain on kitchen paper.

2 Put the tamarind pulp in a bowl with the boiling water and set aside for 20 minutes to soften and dissolve. Strain the liquid through a sieve (discarding the pods and tamarind stones) and place in a pan with the water, fish sauce, caster sugar, pineapple chunks, tomatoes and spring onions. Slowly bring to the boil.

3 If you are using a steamboat, pour the flavoured stock into the hot pan containing smoking coals and add the tiger prawns, squid rings and pieces of fish. Simmer gently for 6–8 minutes.

4 Serve the steamboat while the fish is still cooking, top with coriander and basil leaves, slices of chilli and the deep-fried garlic.

Serves 4–6

8 tablespoons vegetable oil

10 garlic cloves, thinly sliced

1 tablespoon tamarind pulp

150 ml (¼ pint) boiling water

1.2 litres (2 pints) water

2 tablespoons fish sauce

1 teaspoon caster sugar

1 small pineapple, peeled, cored and cut into chunks

175 g (6 oz) tomatoes, quartered

8 spring onions, finely sliced

250 g (8 oz) raw tiger prawns, peeled

3 squid, cleaned and cut into thick rings

250 g (8 oz) rainbow trout fillets, cut into pieces

To serve:

handful of coriander leaves

handful of sweet basil leaves

2 large chillies, diagonally sliced

sour beef, starfruit & pork soup

sinigang, philippines

Sinigang is a classic Philippine dish made with meat or fish, green vegetables and its holy trinity of tomatoes, onions and a sour fruit or vegetable. The souring effect of the fruit has a preservative action, which, in areas where refrigerators still don't exist, is a godsend. In the absence of star fruit (kamias), rhubarb, green mango or unripe guava can be used instead or even lime juice.

1 Place the piece of beef and the pork in a large saucepan with the onion, garlic, tomatoes, star fruit, lemon juice and water. Bring to the boil and skim off all the scum. Reduce the heat and simmer for 1½ hours or until the meat is tender.

2 Remove the beef and pork from the pan and slice thinly. Sieve the stock, pushing the star fruit pulp through the sieve. Return the stock to the saucepan and add the fish sauce and baby pak choi. Simmer for 5–6 minutes then season to taste with salt and pepper.

3 Add the slices of beef and pork to the soup with the radish julienne. Serve with extra fish sauce, lime wedges and pickled green chillies.

Serves 4

375 g (12 oz) piece of braising beef

375 g (12 oz) lean pork

1 onion, finely chopped

2 garlic cloves, crushed

500 g (1 lb) unripe tomatoes, quartered

250 g (8 oz) star fruit (*kamias*), thickly sliced

juice of 1 lemon

1 litre (2 pints) water

3 tablespoons fish sauce

125 g (4 oz) baby pak choi, roughly chopped

75 g (3 oz) white radishes (*daikon*), cut into julienne shreds

salt and pepper

To serve:

fish sauce

lime wedges

pickled green chillies

pepper water

ngayokekaung, burma

No southern Indian, all-you-can-eat lunch would be complete without a pepper water. This Burmese version is sour and tangy and ideal for drinking with Indian and Burmese dry curries such as Burmese Beef & Peanut Curry (see page 56). The mixture of spices, in particular ginger, aids digestion and the soup is surprisingly thirst-quenching.

1 Pour the boiling water over the tamarind pulp and soak for about 20 minutes to soften. Strain through a sieve, pushing any remaining pulp through the sieve. Discard the tamarind stones and pods.

2 Heat the oil in a saucepan and add the chopped onion, garlic and ginger.

3 Heat a small dry frying pan and toast the cumin seeds for 1 minute or until the aroma is released. Cool slightly and grind to a powder in a spice grinder or using a pestle and mortar. Add the ground cumin to the onion mixture with the star anise, dried chillies, turmeric, black pepper and bay leaves and cook over a low heat for about 2 minutes, stirring frequently.

4 Add the tamarind water, vinegar, chicken stock, salt, sugar and water to the pan and simmer gently for 30 minutes

5 Serve in small bowls from which the pepper water can be drunk directly.

Serves 4

150 ml (¼ pint) boiling water

15 g (½ oz) tamarind pulp

3 tablespoons vegetable oil

1 small sweet onion, finely chopped

2 large garlic cloves, crushed

5 cm (2 inch) piece of fresh root ginger, peeled and thinly sliced

2 teaspoons cumin seeds

1 small star anise

2 dried red chillies

½ teaspoon ground turmeric

½ teaspoon ground black pepper

3 bay leaves

1 tablespoon rice wine vinegar

600 ml (1 pint) chicken stock

½ teaspoon salt

½ teaspoon brown sugar

600 ml (1 pint) water

wheat noodle soup with marinated chicken

mohingar, burma

300 g (10 oz) boneless, skinless chicken breasts

1 teaspoon turmeric

2 teaspoons salt

2 lemon grass stalks

3 tablespoons peanuts, skinned and roasted

3 tablespoons white long-grain rice

2 tablespoons vegetable oil

1 onion, chopped

3 garlic cloves, crushed

5 cm (2 inch) piece of fresh root ginger, peeled and finely chopped

¼ teaspoon paprika

2 red bird chillies, chopped

2–3 tablespoons fish sauce

900 ml (1½ pints) water

250 g (8 oz) wheat noodles (*somen*)

To serve:

3 hard-boiled eggs, halved

2 tablespoons chopped coriander leaves

3 spring onions, finely chopped

fish sauce

crushed dried chilli

1–2 tablespoons balachaung (see Glossary page 8)

Mohingar is Burma's answer to Vietnam's pho bo *(see page 12) and China's fish ball* kuaytiaw *soups. Eaten with gusto each morning, from roadside stalls, it is the perfect breakfast food for rehydrating and filling you up. It is without doubt Burma's most common dish. In this version, the fish is substituted with chicken and unless you have a banana plant growing in your garden, the central soft stem of the banana plant trunk* (ngapyawoo) *has to remain an experience a plane ride away.*

1 Cut the chicken breasts into 2.5 cm (1 inch) cubes. Mix the turmeric with the salt and rub into the cubes of chicken and leave to stand for 30 minutes.

2 Bruise the lemon grass with the side of a rolling pin to release the flavour. Finely crush the roasted peanuts in a food processor or using a pestle and mortar. Heat a dry frying pan and toast the rice until golden brown and then finely crush to a powder in a food processor or spice grinder.

3 Heat the oil in a large pan and fry the onion until just softened, add the dry marinated chicken together with the garlic, ginger, lemon grass, paprika and chillies. Add the fish sauce and water and bring to the boil.

4 Reduce the heat and simmer gently. Mix the crushed peanuts and ground rice and add to the pan. Simmer for about 10–15 minutes or until the chicken has cooked through and the broth thickened slightly.

5 Bring a pan of water to the boil and cook the wheat noodles for 3–4 minutes or until just done. Drain and refresh with cold water and then divide between large soup bowls.

6 Ladle the chicken soup over the noodles and serve topped with the hard-boiled eggs, chopped coriander and spring onions. Add an extra splash of fish sauce and a sprinkling of crushed dried chilli and balachaung, to taste. Eat the soup with a spoon and a fork.

Serves 4–6

marinated paneer

tandoori paneer, india

Just off Connaught Circus, at a road-side café in the midst of Delhi's lunchtime chaos, Tandoori Paneer seemed the safest bet. It was my first morning on the Subcontinent. The paneer proved very welcome, nutritious and vegetarian – an excellent choice. For this recipe, you will need 16 wooden skewers. Soak them in water for at least 1 hour before you make the kebabs.

1 Cut the paneer into 1 cm (½ inch) squares.

2 To make the marinade, put the buttermilk into a large bowl with the spices and food colouring, if using, and mix together well. Add the paneer to the marinade, cover and chill overnight.

3 To make the mint raita, mix the chopped mint into the yogurt with the lemon juice. Heat the oil and fry the mustard seeds until they begin to pop, then pour into the raita and stir together.

4 Heat a grill or barbecue. Holding two wooden kebab sticks side by side, thread the pieces of paneer and the green pepper alternately on to the sticks. (Skewering the oblongs of paneer on two sticks helps when turning the kebabs.) Repeat with all the remaining paneer.

5 Brush the kebabs with any remaining marinade and grill for 3–4 minutes on the first side and 2–3 minutes on the second or until beginning to brown.

6 Serve the tandoori paneer with the mint raita and lime wedges.

Serves 4

---

425 g (14 oz) paneer

2 green peppers, cored, deseeded and cut into squares

lime wedges, to serve

Marinade:

300 ml (½ pint) buttermilk or milk

1 teaspoon ground coriander

1 teaspoon ground cumin

1 teaspoon garlic powder

1 teaspoon ground ginger

½ teaspoon dried mint

½ teaspoon chilli powder

1 teaspoon paprika

¼ teaspoon red food colouring (optional)

Mint raita:

3 tablespoons chopped mint

150 ml (¼ pint) thick yogurt

2 teaspoons lemon juice

1 tablespoon vegetable oil

2 teaspoons black or white mustard seeds

potato & fenugreek samosas

samosas, india

Samosas are great snacks, perfect picnic food and truly most excellent with Tamarind Chutney (see page 140). Samosa stalls can be found close to Indian train and bus stations, where samosas, hot out of the oil, are handed to you in leaf bowls held together with a toothpick.

1 To make the pastry, place the flour in a bowl, add the butter and rub in with the fingertips until it resembles fine breadcrumbs. Add the water 1 tablespoon at a time until a soft but firm dough forms. Knead lightly for 5 minutes, then wrap in clingfilm and chill for 1 hour.

2 Heat the vegetable oil, add the onion and cook until soft and beginning to brown. Add the green chilli, turmeric, cumin, coriander and ginger and cook in the oil for 2–3 minutes, stirring constantly. Add the fenugreek leaves and diced potatoes and continue to cook for a further 8–10 minutes, stirring frequently. Remove from the heat and leave to cool.

3 Knead the samosa pastry once more and divide into 12 balls, each about the size of a walnut. Keeping the remaining balls covered with a tea towel, flatten one ball and roll out to a 15 cm (6 inch) circle. Cut the circle in half and form each semi-circle into a cone shape, sealing the edge with water. Fill the cavity with 2 teaspoons of the potato mixture and turn the top side over, again sealing with water. Repeat with the remaining pastry and filling.

4 Heat the oil for deep-frying in a saucepan until a cube of bread browns in 1 minute. Slide 2 samosas into the oil and cook for 2 minutes on one side, turn them over and cook until the second side is golden brown. Remove with a slotted spoon and drain on kitchen paper. Deep-fry the remaining samosas in the same way and serve warm with tamarind or mango chutney.

Makes 24

oil, for deep-frying

Tamarind Chutney (see page 140), or mango chutney, to serve

Pastry:

175 g (6 oz) plain flour

75 g (3 oz) butter

about 4 tablespoons cold water

Filling:

6 tablespoons vegetable oil

1 large onion, finely chopped

1 green chilli, seeds removed and finely chopped

2 teaspoons turmeric

2 teaspoons ground cumin

2 teaspoons ground coriander

2.5 cm (1 inch) piece of fresh root ginger, peeled and grated

125 g (4 oz) fenugreek leaves, chopped, or 2 tablespoons dried fenugreek

375 g (12 oz) potatoes, cut into fine dice

vegetable fritters

pakoras, india

oil, for deep-frying

500 g (1 lb) assorted vegetables: cauliflower florets, slices of sweet potato, thickly sliced onion, segments of red and green peppers, baby aubergines and slices of aubergine

Coriander relish:

25 g (1 oz) coriander leaves, chopped

2 green chillies, finely chopped

4 tablespoons water

1 tablespoon lemon juice

300 ml (½ pint) yogurt

2 teaspoons ground cumin

2 teaspoons caster sugar

1 tablespoon mango chutney

Batter:

125 g (4 oz) chickpea flour (*besan*)

275 ml (9 fl oz) water

½ teaspoon turmeric

½ teaspoon ground cumin

½ teaspoon paprika

½ teaspoon baking soda

Pakoras are a great Indian finger food, served at teatime, at drinks parties and bought from street hawkers on buses and trains. Similar in principle to Japanese tempura, all manner of vegetables can be covered in the batter and deep-fried. Dip them into this Coriander Relish or believe it or not – tomato ketchup!

1 First make the relish. Blend the coriander leaves and green chilli with the water and lemon juice in a food processor. Mix into the yogurt with the ground cumin, sugar and mango chutney. Cover and chill until required.

2 Mix the chickpea flour with enough water to make a smooth and thick batter which will cling to the vegetables. Add the turmeric, cumin, paprika and baking soda and mix together.

3 Heat the oil for deep-frying in a large saucepan until a cube of bread browns in 1 minute. Dip a few vegetables into the batter, then put them straight into the hot oil and deep-fry for 1–2 minutes, depending on their thickness. Remove from the oil and drain on kitchen paper.

4 Serve the pakoras with the coriander relish, while still crisp and warm.

Serves 4–6

thai fish cakes with spicy dipping sauce

tod man plaa, thailand

Little patties of minced fish, served with a Sweet and Sour Cucumber Dipping Sauce, can be found on Thai menus at home, in the market place and as appetizers in some of the grandest of restaurants.

1 Put the red and green chillies, galangal, lemon grass, coriander roots and leaves, lime leaves, garlic, shallots, fish sauce and coriander seeds in a food processor and blend to a smooth paste. Alternatively use a pestle and mortar.

2 Add the fish and blend to a rough paste. Add the egg and sugar and blend once more until smooth.

3 To make the dipping sauce, put the vinegar, sugar, water and fish sauce in a small saucepan and heat until the sugar has dissolved. Remove from the heat, leave to cool then add the cucumber, shallot, carrot and chillies.

4 With damp hands divide the fish mixture into walnut-sized balls and flatten them with the heel of your hand into small fish cakes. Heat the oil for deep-frying until a piece of bread browns in 2 minutes. Add a few fish cakes at a time to the hot oil and cook for 2–3 minutes or until golden brown, turning once.

5 Remove the fish cakes from the oil with a slotted spoon and drain on kitchen paper while frying the remainder. Serve with the dipping sauce.

Serves 4

3 red bird chillies, chopped

2 green bird chillies, chopped

2.5 cm (1 inch) piece of galangal, peeled and finely chopped

1 lemon grass stalk, finely chopped

2 coriander roots, chopped

2 tablespoons chopped coriander leaves

2 kaffir lime leaves, shredded

3 garlic cloves, finely chopped

4 shallots, finely chopped

1 tablespoon fish sauce

1 teaspoon coriander seeds, crushed

500 g (1 lb) white fish fillets, such as cod, haddock or whiting, skinned and roughly chopped

1 small egg, beaten

2 teaspoons palm or brown sugar

oil, for deep frying

Sweet and sour cucumber dipping sauce:

125 ml (4 fl oz) rice vinegar

2 tablespoons caster sugar

2 tablespoons water

2 tablespoons fish sauce

2.5 cm (1 inch) piece cucumber, diced

1 shallot, roughly chopped

1 tablespoon grated carrot

1 red bird chilli, sliced

1 green bird chilli, sliced

1 teaspoon shrimp paste (optional)

4 shallots, finely chopped

6 red bird chillies, finely chopped

2 coriander roots, finely chopped

4 garlic cloves, crushed

2 tablespoons vegetable oil

500 g (1 lb) minced pork

2 firm tomatoes, finely chopped

1 teaspoon brown sugar

4 spring onions, finely sliced

1 tablespoon fish sauce

2 tablespoons chicken stock

handful of chopped coriander
leaves

To serve:

selection of raw vegetables

Thai pork scratchings

northern thai dip

nam prik ong, thailand

Fiery hot and aromatic, this dip is served with vegetables, such as round white or yellow aubergines, yard beans, steamed banana flowers, boiled bamboo shoots, assorted lettuce leaves and large Thai pork scratchings (chitcharon). *Failing any of these, it is equally good with chicory leaves, small sweet Cos lettuce leaves and cherry tomatoes.*

1 Using a pestle and mortar or food processor, blend the shrimp paste, if using, shallots, chillies, coriander roots and garlic to make a paste. Heat the oil in a frying pan until hot and fry the paste for 2–3 minutes to cook the shallots.

2 With the frying pan still searing hot, add the pork to the pan and stir-fry for 5–6 minutes or until the pork is cooked through. Add the tomatoes, sugar, spring onions, fish sauce and chicken stock and simmer for a further 5 minutes.

3 Leave the dip to cool slightly then mix in the chopped coriander. Serve surrounded by a selection of raw vegetables and Thai pork scratchings.

Serves 4–6

sugar cane prawns

chao tom, vietnam

Sugar cane and prawns are readily available in Vietnam. In the West, sugar cane can be bought from some large supermarkets, otherwise go to a large oriental or Indian emporium and ask when they'll next have some in stock. Some of the best sugar cane prawns I tried were in Hoi An, central Vietnam, where many of the old Chinese merchants' houses have opened their doors as restaurants. Either eat the prawns in the traditional way removed from the sugar cane and wrapped in rice paper like a spring roll, or dip them into the sauce and chew from the cane. If sugar cane is hard to find use either lemon grass stalks or bamboo skewers that have been soaked in water.

3 garlic cloves, crushed

500 g (1 lb) raw prawns, peeled

1 teaspoon caster sugar

1 small egg white

25 g (1 oz) pork fat, diced (optional)

1 tablespoon ground toasted rice

30 cm (12 inch) piece of sugar cane

2 tablespoons vegetable oil

Dipping sauce:

2 tablespoons groundnut oil

3 garlic cloves, crushed

3 tablespoons water

1 tablespoon Nuoc Mam Dipping Sauce (see page 94)

1 tablespoon lime juice

2 teaspoons brown sugar

1 tablespoon chopped roasted peanuts

1 small red chilli, finely sliced

To serve:

rice papers (*banh trang*) (see page 32)

assorted lettuce leaves

mint leaves

1 First make the dipping sauce. Heat the oil and lightly fry the garlic until just softened. Add the water, dipping sauce, lime juice and brown sugar and bring to the boil. Remove from the heat and add the peanuts and chilli. Set aside to cool.

2 Using a food processor or a pestle and mortar, blend the garlic and peeled prawns to a smooth paste. Add the sugar, egg white, pork fat, if using, and ground rice and mix well.

3 To make the sugar cane sticks, cut the sugar cane into 10 cm (4 inch) pieces then cut each section into 4 pieces. Cut away the reddish brown outside layer of the sugar cane and discard.

4 Using lightly oiled hands take about 2 tablespoons of the prawn mixture at a time and form into oval balls. Press each ball around a stick of sugar cane. Repeat until all the mixture has been used.

5 Place the sugar cane prawns on a lightly oiled baking sheet and bake in a preheated oven, 180°C (350°F), Gas Mark 4, for 20 minutes, turning once, or grill for 10 minutes.

6 While the prawns are cooking, dampen 8 rice papers and arrange on individual plates with an assortment of lettuce leaves and a small bowl of dipping sauce.

7 Serve the hot sugar cane prawns alongside the wrappers. Allow each person to remove the prawn mixture from the sugar cane and place it, with a selection of lettuce leaves and some mint leaves, inside a piece of rice paper and roll into a cigar shape. Finally dip into the sauce and eat.

Serves 4

satay

saté, thailand

500 g (1 lb) boneless, skinless chicken breasts

4 garlic cloves, crushed

3 red bird chillies, finely chopped

4 shallots, finely chopped

7 cm (3 inch) piece of fresh root ginger, peeled and grated

2 teaspoons ground black pepper

2 tablespoons palm or brown sugar

1 tablespoon soy sauce or kekap manis

2 tablespoons groundnut or vegetable oil

Peanut sauce:

2 tablespoons groundnut oil

125 g (4 oz) roasted peanuts, chopped

2 garlic cloves, crushed

2 shallots, finely chopped

4 red bird chillies, finely chopped

1 kaffir lime leaf

2 tablespoons brown sugar

1 tablespoon lime juice

150 ml (¼ pint) coconut milk

3 tablespoons sweet soy sauce (*kekap manis*) or light soy sauce

To serve:

Pressed Rice (see page 50)

Pickled Cucumber (see page 140)

Satay, succulent little morsels of chicken, beef, duck, seafood or goat are found all over South-east Asia, from Laos, Thailand and Malaysia to Indonesia. Cooked over coals, they are eaten with a lightly spiced peanut sauce, Pressed Rice (see page 50) and Pickled Cucumber (see page 140).

1 Thinly slice the chicken breasts and place in a shallow container. Mix together the garlic, chillies, shallots, ginger, black pepper, sugar, soy sauce and oil and pour over the chicken. Cover the container and leave to marinate for at least 3 hours or overnight. Soak wooden kebab sticks in water for at least 1 hour.

2 Remove the chicken from the marinade and weave the chicken strips on to the kebab sticks. Reserve the marinade.

3 To make the peanut sauce, heat the oil in a pan until hot then add the peanuts, garlic, shallots and chillies and fry for 2–3 minutes or until the shallots have softened. Add the kaffir lime leaf, the sugar, lime juice, coconut milk and soy sauce and simmer for 45 minutes, adding a little water if the sauce becomes too thick.

4 Heat a barbecue or grill. Brush the satay with the marinade and grill for 2–3 minutes on either side. Serve with peanut sauce, Pressed Rice and Pickled Cucumber.

Serves 4

50 g (2 oz) thin cellophane (bean thread) noodles

15 g (½ oz) dried black ear fungus

125 g (4 oz) minced pork

2 shallots, chopped

3 garlic cloves, crushed

2.5 cm (1 inch) piece of fresh root ginger, peeled and finely chopped

½ tablespoon soy sauce

ground black pepper

10 round rice papers (*banh trang*)

2 eggs, beaten

groundnut oil, for deep-frying

sprig of mint, to garnish

Nuoc Mam Dipping Sauce (see page 94), to serve

spring rolls
nem thit, vietnam

Spring rolls are well known as a Chinese starter but these are a little different. The Vietnamese way is to use rice paper as the wrapper – once deep-fried they have a slight opaqueness. Dipped into Nuoc Mam Sauce, spiced up with a little chopped red chilli, they are perfect drinking food. Most Hanoi lunch-time beer houses (bia hois) make large ones and snip them into sections with scissors for better chopstick handling. In southern Vietnam they make them canapé-sized, just right for popping into the mouth in one go.

1 Soak the noodles and fungus in separate bowls of warm water for 20 minutes or until they are soft.

2 Using scissors snip the noodles into 2.5 cm (1 inch) lengths and chop the fungus into small pieces. Mix together with the pork, shallots, garlic, ginger, soy sauce and pepper.

3 With the scissors cut each round of rice paper into 4 quarters. Brush each quarter with egg and leave to soften for a couple of minutes. Place 1 heaped teaspoon of filling towards the rounded edge of the rice paper, fold the sides in and roll up towards the pointed end. Repeat with the remaining filling and rice paper.

4 Heat the oil for deep-frying in a saucepan until a cube of bread browns in 2 minutes. Add about 6 spring rolls and cook for 6–8 minutes or until they are golden brown and the filling cooked through. Repeat with the remaining spring rolls garnish with a sprig of mint and serve with Nuoc Mam Dipping Sauce.

Makes 40

noodles & rice

Rice and noodles are the mainstay of Asian cuisine. A meal would be considered incomplete without a bowl of steamed rice or soup thick with rice or wheat or egg noodles. Rice varies from fragrant Thai rice, the black rice of Indonesia, to sticky glutinous rice which is formed into balls and eaten with the fingers. This type of sticky rice is often found in the north-east of Thailand, Laos and Cambodia. Japanese rice, imperative for making Sushi (see page 46), is similar and slightly sticky. Basmati rice comes from India and is considered the finest quality rice with its long plump grains. It is vital for making a Biriyani (see page 49) or Pulao (see page 45). Noodles also vary greatly, from egg noodles used in Nonya Mie (see page 50), to the soba buckwheat noodles favoured in Japan (see page 38) and the thin and transparent noodles used in Yam Wun Sen (see page 37), the spicy Thai salad.

250 g (8 oz) cellophane (bean thread) noodles

2 tablespoons vegetable oil

175 g (6 oz) minced pork

4 garlic cloves, crushed

1 teaspoon sugar

125 g (4 oz) cooked, peeled prawns

2 shallots, finely sliced

2 tablespoons fish sauce

1 tablespoon lime juice

1 teaspoon caster sugar

2 small red chillies, finely chopped

2 small green chillies, finely chopped

3 tablespoons roasted peanuts, chopped, plus extra to serve

2 tablespoons chopped coriander leaves

To garnish:

2 spring onions, diagonally sliced

1 large red chilli, diagonally sliced

coriander leaves

northern thai salad

yam wun sen, thailand

This crunchy, cold noodle salad has plenty of tanginess and fiery chilli. Around the area of Chiang Mai, it is served with pickled garlic cloves and the very delicious local sausage, which is similar to the Spanish chorizo.

1 Soak the cellophane noodles in warm water for about 20 minutes. Drain well and, using a pair of scissors, snip them into shorter lengths.

2 Heat the oil in a frying pan and fry the pork until cooked through. Add the garlic and sugar and stir-fry for 3 minutes.

3 Remove from the heat and stir the pork mixture into the noodles. Add the prawns, shallots, fish sauce, lime juice, sugar, chillies, peanuts and coriander. Toss the ingredients together and serve in heaped portions, garnished with spring onions, red chilli and coriander leaves. Serve with the extra chopped roasted peanuts.

Serves 4

buckwheat noodles
& sea bream

tai no shinshu-mushi, japan

Simplicity and top quality ingredients typify this Japanese dish. Buckwheat noodles (soba) are a speciality of the wheat growing Shinshu region of mainland Japan. They are available in this original form or as a green version flavoured with green tea.

500 g (1 lb) sea bream, scaled, gutted and filleted

2 teaspoons salt

2 sheets kombu seaweed

500 g (1 lb) soba noodles

8 tablespoons sake

6 tablespoons dark soy sauce

6 tablespoons mirin

15 g (½ oz) dried tuna flakes (*bonito*)

To serve:

6 thin spring onions, finely sliced

small piece of nori seaweed, toasted and crumbled

1 With the flesh of the fish uppermost, rub the salt into the fillets and set aside for 20 minutes to allow the flesh to firm up.

2 Cut the kombu seaweed into 4 pieces and use to line 4 small plates. Bring a pan of water to the boil and add the noodles. Cook for 5 minutes or until just tender.

3 Drain the noodles and divide between the plates lined with seaweed. Cut each fish fillet into 2 and place skin side up on the noodles. Pour a tablespoon of sake over each fish fillet, cover with clingfilm and place in a steamer over boiling water for 8–10 minutes.

4 Put the remaining sake, the soy sauce, and mirin into a small saucepan and bring to the boil. Immediately remove from the heat and add the tuna flakes. Strain after 5 minutes and discard the tuna flakes.

5 Remove the clingfilm from the fish and noodles and pour a little sauce over the fish. Add a mound of spring onion and a sprinkling of nori seaweed to each portion.

Serves 4

char siu pork over rice

khao muu daeng, thailand

All over South-east Asia Char Siu Pork over Rice (khao muu daeng, as they call it in Thailand), is served as a quick lunch or supper. In Thailand small eateries can be recognised by the char siu pork fillets hanging in the window beside the roasted duck. When you have ordered, the fillet is thinly sliced and served over warm Thai rice, and a ladleful of hot and sweet sauce is poured over the top. Eat with iced green tea (nam cha).

1 First mix together all the marinade ingredients. Put the pork fillet into a container and pour the marinade over. Cover and chill overnight.

2 Preheat the oven to 200°C (400°F), Gas Mark 6. Remove the fillet from the marinade, reserve the marinade, and place the pork fillet on a wire rack set over a baking sheet. Brush the fillet with some of the reserved marinade and roast in the centre of the preheated oven for 20 minutes.

3 To make the sauce, put the reserved marinade into a saucepan with the stock, rice wine and salt. Bring to the boil, stirring constantly, and simmer for 5 minutes. Mix the cornflour with a little water until a smooth paste is formed and add to the sauce. Stir constantly until the sauce thickens.

4 To serve, slice the pork thinly and arrange on a plate of steaming rice with the slices of cucumber. Pour a little sauce over the pork. Top with deep-fried shallots and garlic and a few coriander leaves.

Serves 4

500 g (1 lb) pork fillet

375 g (12 oz) freshly cooked basmati rice

Marinade:

1 teaspoon five spice powder

3 tablespoons shaoxing rice wine

2 tablespoons brown sugar

1 tablespoon dark soy sauce

1½ tablespoons hoisin sauce

2 tablespoons rice vinegar

2 tablespoons honey

red food colouring (optional)

Sauce:

150 ml (¼ pint) chicken stock

3 tablespoons shaoxing rice wine

½ teaspoon salt

1 teaspoon cornflour

To serve:

cucumber, thickly sliced

2 tablespoons deep-fried shallots (see page 8)

2 tablespoons deep-fried garlic (see page 8)

coriander leaves

coconut rice

ohnhtamin, burma

This rice dish is cooked for special days, such as the Burmese Buddhist monk initiation ceremony in Naungshwe, in the north-east Shan state. It accompanies a variety of dry curries such as Burmese Beef & Peanut Curry (see page 56) and can be served with a sesame seasoning (nhandaung).

1 To make the sesame seasoning, heat a dry heavy-based pan, add the sesame seeds and salt and dry-fry for 4 minutes, stirring constantly. Once the sesame seeds are golden brown, remove the pan from the heat and grind them to a powder.

2 Place the rice, coconut milk, onion, sugar and salt in a large saucepan and tap the pan to level the surface of the rice. Cover with enough water to reach 2.5 cm (1 inch) above the rice. Bring the pan to the boil, then reduce the heat, cover with a lid and simmer very gently for 20 minutes adding a little extra water, if necessary, and carefully stirring the rice once or twice to prevent it from sticking to the bottom of the pan. To serve, fluff the rice with a fork and sprinkle with a little sesame seasoning.

Serves 4–6

500 g (1 lb) basmati rice
475 ml (16 fl oz) coconut milk
1 onion, halved and sliced
2 teaspoons caster sugar
½ teaspoon salt

Sesame seasoning (*nhandaung*):
4 tablespoons sesame seeds
1 teaspoon salt

chilli chicken with udon noodles

kake udon, japan

A hearty dish that relies on a superior broth, perfectly cooked udon noodles and marinated chicken. Serve with extra bean sprouts and a light chilli sauce, for those who love the almighty chilli.

1 Mix together the chilli sauce, soy sauce, mirin and teriyaki sauce and spread over the chicken breasts. Cover and leave to marinate for 2–3 hours.

2 Slowly bring the stock to the boil. Cook the udon noodles in boiling salted water for 1–2 minutes. Drain well and set aside.

3 Heat a griddle or heavy-based frying pan and cook the chicken on both sides for about 10 minutes or until cooked through. Remove from the heat, leave to stand for 5 minutes and then slice widthways.

4 Divide the noodles between 4 soup bowls. Ladle the stock over the noodles, add the pak choi, onion, bean sprouts and parsley and then arrange the chicken slices on top.

5 Mix together the rice vinegar, sugar and chilli oil and serve in small bowls. Serve the soup with soy sauce, wedges of lime and topped with deep-fried garlic.

Serves 4

2 tablespoons chilli sauce

2 tablespoons soy sauce

½ tablespoon mirin

1 tablespoon teriyaki sauce

4 chicken breasts, skinned

1.2 litres (2 pints) chicken stock

375 g (12 oz) fresh udon noodles

125 g (4 oz) baby pak choi, quartered

1 sweet onion, finely sliced

75 g (3 oz) bean sprouts

2 tablespoons chopped flat leaf parsley

6 tablespoons rice vinegar

½ teaspoon caster sugar

1 tablespoon chilli oil

To serve:

soy sauce, to taste

thick lime wedges

1 tablespoon deep-fried garlic (see page 8)

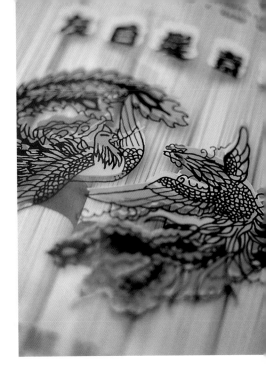

laksa

laksa lemak, malaysia

3 tablespoons groundnut oil

2 large onions, finely chopped

4 garlic cloves, crushed

3 red bird chillies, finely chopped

75 g (3 oz) roasted peanuts, chopped

1 tablespoon ground coriander

1 tablespoon ground cumin

2 teaspoons turmeric

1.2 litres (2 pints) coconut milk

1 teaspoon shrimp paste

1–2 tablespoons sugar, to taste

375 g (12 oz) cooked chicken, shredded

175 g (6 oz) bean sprouts

500 g (1 lb) fresh flat rice noodles

4 spring onions, chopped

3 tablespoons chopped coriander leaves

salt and pepper

To serve:

spring onions, chopped

1 large red chilli, finely sliced

1–2 tablespoons chopped roasted peanuts

This rich and creamy coconut concoction is a main course in itself. It is made with fine bean thread vermicelli in the Philippines and flat rice noodles in Malaysia. Finish it off with chopped spring onion, extra fresh and dried chilli and roasted peanuts.

1 Heat the oil and fry the onions until golden brown. Add the garlic, chillies, peanuts, ground coriander, cumin and turmeric and fry for 2–3 minutes or until the spices have cooked through and released a strong aroma.

2 Stir the coconut milk and shrimp paste into the spice mixture, cover the pan and leave to simmer for 15 minutes. Season the spiced coconut with salt, pepper and sugar to taste. Add the shredded chicken and half of the bean sprouts to the coconut mixture and simmer for 5 minutes.

3 Blanch the fresh noodles in boiling water and divide between 4 large bowls. Sprinkle with the spring onions and chopped coriander and divide the remaining raw bean sprouts between the bowls.

4 Ladle the chicken and coconut mixture over the noodles and serve with chopped spring onions, red chilli and roasted peanuts.

Serves 4

sour rice

bibimbap, korea

3 tablespoons oil

250 g (8 oz) freshly cooked
Japanese rice (see page 46)

125 g (4 oz) rump steak, cut into
strips

75 g (3 oz) bean sprouts

4 spring onions, thinly sliced

2 carrots, cut into julienne strips

1 sheet nori seaweed, toasted and
shredded

4–6 fried eggs

2 teaspoons caster sugar

2 tablespoons sesame oil

2 teaspoons sesame seeds

Rice with all the trimmings: this Korean dish is traditionally cooked in a clay pot (tukbaege) and accompanied by the Korean speciality, pickled cabbage (kimchi). True to its original form, it is cooked here with all the flavouring ingredients layered on top of the rice but a more contemporary presentation usually finds them carefully mixed together.

1 Rub the bottom and sides of a heavy-based pan or individual clay pots with some of the oil and add the steaming rice. Cover the pan or pots with a lid, place over a medium heat and cook gently for 5 minutes.

2 Heat the remaining oil in a frying pan and quickly stir-fry the beef for 1 minute. Remove from the heat and arrange over the rice with the bean sprouts, spring onions, carrots, shredded nori and the fried eggs. Replace the lid and cook for a further 5 minutes.

3 In a small pan, gently heat the sugar in the sesame oil until the sugar has dissolved. Spoon this mixture over the fried eggs and rice and sprinkle with the sesame seeds. Serve immediately.

Serves 4–6

spicy fried rice

nasi goreng, indonesia

3 tablespoons vegetable oil

3 shallots, sliced

2 garlic cloves, thinly sliced

50 g (2 oz) green or white cabbage,
shredded

1–2 red chillies, finely chopped

1 green chilli, finely chopped

175 g (6 oz) chicken breast, diced

425 g (14 oz) cold cooked rice

75 g (3 oz) cooked, peeled prawns

3 tablespoons dark soy sauce or
ketchup manis

1 teaspoon caster sugar

1 tablespoon chopped parsley

To serve:

1 tablespoon deep-fried shallots

coriander leaves

prawn crackers (*krupuk*)

One of the most popular dishes in Malaysia and Indonesia, this is simply a Chinese-style fried rice dish. A moveable feast, it is served at breakfast time topped with a fried egg and for lunch or supper, dressed with slices of beef, chicken or dried prawns. Serve with Sambal (see page 74).

1 Heat the oil until very hot in a wok or large frying pan and add the shallots, garlic, cabbage, red and green chillies and stir-fry for 1 minute.

2 Add the chicken and stir-fry for 2 minutes or until it has cooked through. Add the rice and prawns and stir-fry over a high heat for 3–4 minutes.

3 Add the soy sauce, caster sugar and chopped parsley and stir-fry for 1 minute.

4 Serve piled high on a plate, topped with deep-fried shallots, coriander leaves and prawn crackers.

Serves 4

sticky rice

khao niew, thailand

500 g (1 lb) glutinous rice

This is the typical rice of Laos and the north and north-east (Issan) region of Thailand. Here they eat with their fingers, and sticky rice is the perfect vehicle with which to scoop up food and pop it into the mouth. It is traditionally served with Larb (see page 119).

1 Put the rice into a large bowl and cover with plenty of cold water and leave to soak overnight.

2 Drain the rice and place in a steamer lined with muslin or a double thickness of kitchen paper. Place over a pan of boiling water and steam for 30 minutes, covered.

3 Remove from the heat and allow to stand for 10 minutes before turning out on to a tray and breaking up any lumps with a spatula. Return the rice to a covered container until ready to serve. Pull off pieces of rice and mould in the hand before eating.

Serves 4–6

rice with raisins & cashews

pulao, india

1 tablespoon ghee or vegetable oil

2 large onions, thinly sliced

½ teaspoon salt

5 g (¼ oz) cassia bark or cinnamon stick

6 green cardamoms or 2 large black cardamoms, bruised

½ teaspoon black peppercorns

½ teaspoon cumin seeds

½ teaspoon fennel seeds

500 g (1 lb) basmati rice, washed

25 g (1 oz) sultanas

50 g (2 oz) toasted cashew nuts, chopped

Pulao rice is highly aromatic and ideal with any north Indian or Burmese curry. Originating from Persia, the spices delicately flavour the rice and the base of the rice is often crispy. It is a perfect accompaniment to tandoori meat or fish with a cucumber and mint raita and mango chutney.

1 Heat the ghee or oil in a large saucepan, add the onions and fry until golden brown and crisp. Remove half of the onions and reserve.

2 Add the salt and all the spices and stir in the hot oil for 1–2 minutes or until the aroma of the spices is released. Add the rice and coat in the oil.

3 Level the surface of the rice and pour in enough water to reach 1 cm (½ inch) above the rice. Bring the water to the boil, then reduce the heat, cover the pan and simmer for 20 minutes.

4 Remove the pan from the heat and add the sultanas and cashew nuts. Set aside to stand, covered, for 10 minutes, then fluff with a fork. Turn out the rice on to a warmed platter and scatter with the remaining fried onions.

Serves 4–6

nigiri sushi

japan

500 g (1 lb) Japanese short-grain rice, rinsed

575 ml (18 fl oz) cold water

25 g (1 oz) sugar

1 tablespoon salt

4 tablespoons Japanese rice vinegar

2 tablespoons wasabi paste

500 g (1 lb) assorted prepared seafood: thin slices of fresh tuna, salmon, mackerel, scored cooked squid, shelled deveined cooked prawns

To serve:

pickled ginger

wasabi

soy sauce

This is one of the easiest and most popular forms of sushi to make at home. Shape the rice when cool and top with a selection of the freshest fish available.

1 Put the rice in a heavy-based saucepan with the cold water. Cover the pan, bring to the boil and simmer for 20 minutes or until the rice is tender and the water absorbed. Remove from the heat, cover the pan with a tea towel and leave to stand for 10 minutes.

2 Put the sugar, salt and vinegar into a small saucepan and heat gently until the sugar has dissolved.

3 Turn the rice out of the pan into a large bowl, sprinkle with the sweetened vinegar and toss gently with two forks to mix the vinegar dressing into the rice and to separate the grains as they cool.

4 Once cool, shape walnut-sized balls of rice into ovals with wet hands. Spread a little wasabi over the top of the shaped rice and arrange a piece of fish or seafood on the top. Arrange on a platter and serve with pickled ginger, extra wasabi and soy sauce.

Serves 6–8

rice ball sushi

onigiri, japan

1 quantity cooked Japanese rice (see above)

75 g (3 oz) raw salmon, diced

1–2 teaspoons wasabi paste

1 teaspoon pickled ginger

2 tablespoons sesame seeds, toasted

1 sheet nori seaweed

To serve:

Japanese soy sauce

pickled pink ginger

Hand-pressed sushi containing hidden titbits such as wasabi, raw salmon and pickled ginger and wrapped in a cuff of toasted nori seaweed are perfect for lunch, light suppers or as a canapé with drinks.

1 Put 2 tablespoons of cooked rice in a damp Japanese or Chinese tea cup or an egg cup. Make a well in the centre for the filling.

2 Add a little raw salmon, wasabi and pickled ginger and press a little more rice over the top to seal. With wet hands shake the rice from the cup and mould lightly into a round. Sprinkle with sesame seeds. Repeat with the remaining rice and filling.

3 Toast the sheet of nori seaweed over a flame and then, using scissors, cut it into 2.5 cm (1 inch) strips.

4 Wrap a strip of nori around each rice ball, sealing the ends of the seaweed together with a little water. Chill for a couple of hours or serve immediately with soy sauce and pickled ginger.

Serves 6–8

chicken biryani

murgh biryani, india

Brought by the Moghuls to India and Burma, this is a very elaborate dish that is cooked at home for special feast days and depending on the occasion might be decorated with silver leaf. Otherwise people go out to sample it, and in Yangon (Rangoon), in Burma, a stretch of Anawrahta Road is devoted to biryani restaurants.

1 First make the marinade. Blend the garlic, ginger, onion, cloves, peppercorns, the seeds from the cardamon pods, coriander and cumin seeds, turmeric and mace to make a spice paste. Fry the paste in the oil for 2–3 minutes. Leave to cool then stir into the yogurt and spread over the chicken pieces. Cover and leave to marinate for a minimum of 3 hours or overnight.

2 Heat the oil in a large casserole. Remove the chicken from the marinade and brown on all sides, remove from the heat and add the left over marinade.

3 Soak the saffron in the hot milk. Put the rice into a large saucepan. Cover with water and bring to the boil, then reduce the heat and simmer for 5 minutes. The rice will not be cooked. Drain well and place on top of the chicken. Add the cassia bark or cinnamon stick, bay leaves, and the bruised cardamon pods.

4 Pour the saffron threads and milk and the stock over the rice, cover the casserole with a tight-fitting lid and cook in a preheated oven, 150°C (300°F), Gas Mark 2, for 1 hour. About 10 minutes before the dish is ready, put the sultanas and almonds on the top of the rice.

5 To serve, spoon the rice and chicken on to a warm plate and serve with the fried onion, extra toasted almonds and sultanas, and garnish with silver leaf.

Serves 4–6

1.5 kg (3 lb) chicken, cut into 8 joints

2 tablespoons vegetable oil or ghee

10 saffron threads

300 ml (½ pint) hot milk

500 g (1 lb) basmati rice

15 g (½ oz) cassia bark or cinnamon stick, broken up

2 bay leaves

6 cardamom pods, bruised

150 ml (¼ pint) chicken stock

75 g (3 oz) sultanas

50 g (2 oz) toasted almonds

edible silver leaf, to garnish

Marinade:

5 garlic cloves, crushed

7.5 cm (3 inch) piece of fresh root ginger, peeled and chopped

1 onion, chopped

1 teaspoon cloves

1 teaspoon black peppercorns

3 cardamom pods, bruised

1 tablespoon coriander seeds

1 tablespoon cumin seeds

½ teaspoon turmeric

2 pieces mace

2 tablespoons vegetable oil or ghee

300 ml (½ pint) thick Greek yogurt

To serve:

2 onions, sliced and deep-fried

1 tablespoon toasted almonds

½ tablespoon sultanas

2 tablespoons vegetable oil

1 onion, chopped

3 garlic cloves, crushed

2 tablespoons black bean sauce, plus extra to serve

2 tablespoons Chinese rice wine

1 red chilli, finely chopped

½ teaspoon Chinese five spice powder

600 ml (1 pint) chicken stock or water

250 g (8 oz) fresh egg noodles

150 g (5 oz) bean sprouts

250 g (8 oz) roasted Char Siu Pork (see page 39), sliced

125 g (4 oz) pak choi, bok choi or mustard greens, roughly chopped

125 g (4 oz) peeled raw tiger prawns

½ teaspoon salt

To serve:

6 shallots, thinly sliced and deep-fried

2 egg omelette, thinly shredded

2 red chillies, diagonally sliced

coriander leaves

Sweet Chilli Sauce (see page 141)

singaporean noodles

nonya mie, singapore

The Nonya people who are also known as the Straits Chinese, are of mixed Chinese and Malay ancestry. Their origins go back to the times of the trading routes when the Chinese merchants came to Malaysia to trade. Here they took local wives, and the Nonya way of life, which encompasses both cultures from styles of dress right down to types of food, was born. Today the Nonya community is most in evidence in Malacca on the west coast of Malaysia, where a few Nonya restaurants, housed in the old homes of the grandest merchants, serve some of these delicious dishes.

1 Heat the oil in a wok or large frying pan. Add the onion and stir-fry until beginning to brown. Add the garlic, black bean sauce, rice wine, chilli, and Chinese five spice powder and stir-fry for 2 minutes.

2 Add the stock or water, noodles and bean sprouts and bring to the boil, tossing the noodles and bean sprouts in the stock.

3 Add the pork to the wok with the green vegetables, the prawns and salt and stir-fry for a further 4 minutes. Serve topped with the deep-fried shallots, the shredded omelette, sliced chillies and coriander leaves and accompanied by sweet chilli sauce.

Serves 4

375 g (12 oz) long-grain rice

600 ml (1 pint) water

½ teaspoon salt

2 pandanus or screwpine leaves (optional)

pressed rice

nasi empet, indonesia

Rice is served in some form at almost every meal in Asia. In Indonesia, Malaysia and Thailand, this pressed rice is served with satay to make it into a substantial dish. These small cakes of rice are sometimes served with Indonesian Beef Rendang (see page 57).

1 Rinse the rice and place it in a large saucepan with the water, salt and pandanus leaves, if using, and bring to the boil. Reduce the heat and simmer for 20 minutes or until the rice is tender and the water absorbed.

2 Remove the pan from the heat, stir the rice with a fork to break up any lumps, then discard the leaves and spoon the rice into a large tray or baking tin. Smooth the surface, cover with muslin or clingfilm and place a tray or tin of similar size on top. Use weights to press the rice down in the tin. Chill overnight until firm and then cut it into small oblong pieces with a sharp knife.

Serves 6–8

curries

Curries are a favourite throughout South-east Asia, Burma and India. Hot and spicy, they are often given a distinctive tanginess by the addition of tamarind or lemon juice. The rich creaminess of coconut frequently tempers the heat of red and green chillies as in the Malaysian influenced Musaman Curry (see page 69), south Indian Malabar Fish Curry (see page 61) and tangy Aubergine and Beef Tamarind Curry (see page 54).

aubergine & beef tamarind curry

samlaa ko phet, cambodia

Cambodian cooking contains elements from the cooking of the countries that surround it – Thailand, Vietnam and Laos. This beef curry uses all the usual South-east Asian ingredients, the tart tamarind, scented lemon grass, pungent fish sauce and hot bird chillies. I first sampled a version of this dish at Wild Ginger, an oriental restaurant in Seattle, USA, where there is a growing Cambodian and Vietnamese community.

3 red bird chillies, chopped

1 lemon grass stalk, chopped

5 cm (2 inch) piece of fresh galangal, peeled and sliced

3 coriander roots, finely chopped

3 tablespoons vegetable oil

4 shallots, finely chopped

3 large garlic cloves, crushed

500 g (1 lb) sirloin beef, sliced

150 ml (¼ pint) Tamarind Water (see page 9)

4 kaffir lime leaves, shredded

1 teaspoon shrimp paste

300 ml (½ pint) coconut milk

150 ml (¼ pint) beef stock or water

1 teaspoon caster sugar

1–2 tablespoons fish sauce, to taste

125 g (4 oz) pea aubergines or larger green aubergines, quartered

1 large red chilli, deseeded and finely chopped

juice of 1 lime

10–15 sweet basil leaves

mint sprigs, to garnish

1 Place the chillies, lemon grass, galangal and coriander roots in a food processor and blend to a smooth paste.

2 Heat the oil in a saucepan and fry the shallots and garlic for 2–3 minutes. Add the spice paste and fry for a further 2–3 minutes.

3 Add the beef to the pan and sear on all sides. Add the tamarind water, kaffir lime leaves, shrimp paste, coconut milk, stock, sugar and fish sauce. Simmer for 20 minutes.

4 Add the aubergines to the pan with the chopped red chilli, lime juice and basil leaves and simmer for 5 minutes. Garnish with mint sprigs.

Serves 4

burmese beef & peanut curry

ahmaithar ohno hin, burma

I first ate a version of this curry in Nyaungshwe, in the Shan state of north-east Burma, while staying with the highly amusing Pyi, who runs a local guesthouse. Nyaungshwe is at the northern end of Inle lake, a vast, dead calm lake dotted with floating market gardens – literally patches of floating vegetation. Pyi's family cooks a series of Shan dishes to accompany an evening of local dancing, also performed by members of his family. This Shan dish is often accompanied by bean soup, fish curry, fried peanuts and Coconut Rice (see page 40) and is traditionally assembled in a large lacquerware bowl.

1 Mix the salt, flour and turmeric together and sprinkle over the beef cubes in a bowl. Heat the oil in a large heavy-based frying pan and fry the onions until softened.

2 Add the garlic, paprika, ground coriander, garam masala, ginger and lemon grass and cook for 3–4 minutes or until the onion has browned. Remove from the pan. Add the beef, a few pieces at a time, and brown on all sides.

3 Return the onions and spices to the pan. Add the coconut, with the soaking water if applicable, the measured water and the tomatoes. Cover and simmer very gently for 1½–2 hours until the sauce has reduced to a thick sauce and the meat is tender. Season to taste with salt and pepper. Serve sprinkled with peanuts and balachaung.

Serves 4–6

1 teaspoon salt

1 tablespoon plain flour

2 teaspoons turmeric

1 kg (2 lb) braising beef, cubed

4 tablespoons vegetable oil

3 onions, finely chopped

4 garlic cloves, crushed

1 teaspoon paprika

1 tablespoon ground coriander

2 tablespoons garam masala

7.5 cm (3 inch) piece of fresh root ginger, peeled and finely chopped

1 lemon grass stalk, finely chopped

flesh from 1 coconut, grated, or 50 g (2 oz) desiccated coconut, soaked in warm water for 30 minutes

900 ml (1½ pints) water

4 tomatoes, quartered

salt and pepper

To serve:

3 tablespoons roasted peanuts, chopped

2 tablespoons balachaung (see Glossary page 8)

beef rendang

rendang sapi, indonesia

Rendang is considered to be the most important Indonesian dish and is eaten all over the Indonesian archipelago but in fact it comes from west Sumatra. It is one of the most popular dishes offered in a Padang restaurant, where a selection of dishes is brought to the table in saucers and the diner decides which they wish to eat. The bill depends on the quantity consumed. Hot, spicy and dry, a rendang's flavour improves with long slow cooking, as well as being kept for a couple of days in the refrigerator. The starting point of this dish is the preparation of the coconut: a series of sharp blows with the back of a cleaver, all the way round the coconut. This is repeated again and again and eventually the two halves fall apart. It really works but take care. The flesh is then grated and used to make coconut milk. Here in the West, cans of coconut milk are far easier to open and readily available.

1 Put 1 teaspoon of the salt, the turmeric, chilli powder, garlic, ginger, galangal, peppercorns, cardamoms and chillies in a food processor and process until roughly chopped or pound in a mortar with a pestle. Add the lemon grass and onions and process to a dry paste. Add the tamarind water and blend to a soft paste.

2 Heat the oil in a large saucepan and fry the beef until browned on all sides. Remove with a slotted spoon and reserve.

3 Add the spice paste to the hot pan and fry for 2–3 minutes, stirring constantly. Return the beef to the pan with all the remaining ingredients and bring slowly to the boil, stirring constantly.

4 Reduce the heat and simmer very gently for 4–4½ hours, stirring occasionally, until the meat is tender and the sauce has reduced and thickened.

5 When the sauce is very thick, increase the heat and, stirring constantly, fry the beef in the thick sauce until the meat is a rich brown colour.

Serves 4–6

1½ teaspoons salt

1 teaspoon turmeric

½ teaspoon chilli powder

6 garlic cloves, chopped

5 cm (2 inch) piece of fresh root ginger, peeled and grated

5 cm (2 inch) piece of fresh galangal, peeled and grated

1 teaspoon black peppercorns, roughly crushed

4 cardamom pods, bruised

4 red chillies, chopped

1 lemon grass stalk, finely chopped

3 large onions, finely chopped

2 tablespoons Tamarind Water (see page 9)

3 tablespoons coconut or vegetable oil

750 g (1½ lb) braising beef, sliced

900 ml (1½ pints) coconut milk

150 ml (¼ pint) water

1 tablespoon dark brown sugar

4 kaffir lime leaves, shredded

3 star anise

1 large cinnamon stick

750 g (1½ lb) pork fillet, thinly sliced

1 teaspoon chilli powder

1 teaspoon turmeric

3 tablespoons vegetable oil

2 onions, chopped

6 garlic cloves, crushed

2 lemon grass stalks, finely chopped

5 cm (2 inch) piece of fresh galangal
or fresh root ginger, peeled and
sliced

2 red chillies, chopped

1 teaspoon shrimp paste

6 tablespoons Tamarind Water
(see page 9)

300 ml (½ pint) chicken stock or
water

175 g (6 oz) can bamboo shoots,
drained

1–2 tablespoons ground fish
(optional)

salt and pepper

To serve:

2–3 tablespoons balachaung

(see Glossary page 8)

handful of coriander leaves

pork & bamboo shoots in thick sauce

whetthar myitchin hin, burma

This is an everyday pork dish that is served at home as part of a simple family meal with a soup, a vegetable dish, plain rice and green tea. Most Burmese would eat this with their fingers. For the best flavour choose fresh bamboo shoots from oriental stores. They are kept in large plastic buckets, covered with water and ready for individual selection.

1 Place the pork fillet in a bowl. Mix the chilli powder and turmeric together and rub into the sliced pork. Set aside for 30 minutes to allow the spices to flavour the pork.

2 Heat the oil and gently fry the onions and garlic for 10–15 minutes or until golden brown. Add the lemon grass, galangal, red chillies and shrimp paste and fry for 2–3 minutes, stirring constantly.

3 Add the pork to the spice mixture and fry on all sides for 3–4 minutes or until the meat has sealed. Add the tamarind water and stock and simmer for 8 minutes.

4 Stir in the bamboo shoots, the ground fish, if using, and season with salt and pepper. Simmer gently for 5 minutes. Serve with balachaung and coriander leaves.

Serves 4

chicken shakuti

murgh xaccutti, india

Xaccutti is a Goanese speciality; it is rich and coconutty, with a sour tang from lemon juice. In the deep south of Goa, on the coastal road running north out of Benaulim, there is a small restaurant called Sidel's Dream. Here Sidel's mother and grandmother cook exceptional local dishes including this Chicken Shakuti.

1 Spread the chillies, cumin, coriander seeds and fenugreek seeds, peppercorns and cloves over the surface of a baking sheet and roast in a preheated oven, 200°C (400°F), Gas Mark 6, for 5 minutes. Allow to cool slightly then grind to a powder with the cardamom seeds and cinnamon. Add the turmeric.

2 Heat the oil in a saucepan and fry the onions and garlic until softened and beginning to brown. Add the spice mixture and toasted coconut and fry, stirring constantly, for 1 minute.

3 Add the chicken to the pan and seal in the oil. Add the peanuts, coconut milk and stock and simmer gently for 40 minutes.

4 Once the chicken has cooked through and is tender, add the lemon juice and salt. Simmer for 5 minutes, then serve.

Serves 4

3 dried Kashmiri chillies

2 teaspoons ground cumin

1 tablespoon coriander seeds

1 teaspoon fenugreek seeds

½ teaspoon peppercorns

½ teaspoon cloves

4 cardamom pods, seeds removed

1 small cinnamon stick

1 teaspoon turmeric

3 tablespoons vegetable oil

2 onions, finely chopped

3 garlic cloves, crushed

50 g (2 oz) desiccated coconut, toasted

1.5 kg (3 lb) chicken, jointed

25 g (1 oz) roasted peanuts, roughly chopped

150 ml (¼ pint) coconut milk

150 ml (¼ pint) chicken stock

juice of 2 lemons

½ teaspoon salt

pork vindaloo

vindaloo, india

This dish dates back to the days when the Portuguese who ruled Goa introduced the chilli and tomato to its culinary repertoire. A chilli hot dish, the sour taste comes from tamarind and from vinegar, which is used extensively in Goanese cooking and is added at the end of recipes for a more pointed and balancing effect.

1 Soak the dried chillies in water for 30 minutes to soften. Put them into a food processor with the green chillies, cayenne pepper, cumin seeds and black peppercorns and blend to a semi-smooth paste, or use a pestle and mortar. Spread 1 tablespoon of the spice paste over the cubed pork, cover and leave to marinate for 2–3 hours.

2 Heat the oil and fry the onions and garlic for 10 minutes or until golden brown and caramelized. Add the remaining spice paste and fry, stirring constantly, for 3–4 minutes. Increase the heat and add the marinated pork and seal the meat on all sides.

3 Add the ginger, curry leaves, sugar, tamarind water and stock and simmer for 40 minutes, or until the meat is tender. Season to taste with salt and pepper, stir in the vinegar and simmer for a further 5 minutes. Serve with plain, boiled basmati rice.

Serves 6

10 dried red Kashmiri chillies

3 green chillies

2 teaspoons cayenne pepper

1 teaspoon cumin seeds

1 teaspoon black peppercorns

1 kg (2 lb) shoulder of pork, cubed

3 tablespoons vegetable oil

2 large onions, chopped

4 garlic cloves, crushed

7.5 cm (3 inch) piece of fresh root ginger, peeled and finely chopped

8 curry leaves

2 teaspoons brown sugar

150 ml (¼ pint) Tamarind Water (see page 9)

300 ml (½ pint) chicken stock or water

1½ tablespoons white wine vinegar

salt and pepper

basmati rice, to serve

malabar fish curry

moolee, india

On the south-west coast of India, south of Goa, is the state of Kerala. This fertile stretch of land is known as the Malabar coast and has a wealth of produce including home-grown spices, coconuts and, of course, plenty of fish. The chilli and the coconut are vital to this region's cooking. In Cochin old town just such a fish and seafood curry, bathed in coconut milk and finished with a Coconut Sambal (see page 63), is served at the Malabar Residency, a fine new hotel set in an old colonial house.

1 Mix the chilli powder, turmeric, mustard seeds, cinnamon and garlic and rub into the fish and prawns. Cover and leave for a couple of hours to dry-marinate in the refrigerator.

2 Heat the oil and fry the ginger, chillies and onions for 5 minutes to soften and slightly brown. Add the pieces of marinated fish and fry lightly on both sides. Add any remaining spice mixture together with the curry leaves, then stir in the coconut milk and stock and simmer very gently for 8 minutes.

3 Add the marinated prawns and simmer for a further 5 minutes. Season to taste with salt and pepper and garnish with chopped coriander. Serve with chapatis.

Serves 4–6

1 tablespoon chilli powder

1 teaspoon turmeric

½ teaspoon yellow mustard seeds

½ teaspoon ground cinnamon

4 large garlic cloves, crushed

750 g (1½ lb) swordfish, tuna, shark or haddock, cut into thick steaks

125 g (4 oz) raw tiger prawns

2 tablespoons coconut or vegetable oil

2.5 cm (1 inch) piece of fresh root ginger, peeled and finely chopped

2 green chillies, finely chopped

2 onions, finely chopped

10–15 curry leaves

450 ml (¾ pint) coconut milk

150 ml (¼ pint) fish stock or water

salt and pepper

2 tablespoons finely chopped coriander, to garnish

chapatis, to serve

sri lankan seafood curry

maach kari, sri lanka

500 g (1 lb) fish such as tuna, swordfish, mackerel, pomfret or haddock, skin and bones removed, and roughly cubed

3 tablespoons groundnut or vegetable oil

2 onions, finely chopped

4 garlic cloves, crushed

1 lemon grass stalk, bruised

2.5 cm (1 inch) piece of fresh root ginger, finely chopped

2 teaspoons turmeric

6–8 curry leaves

400 g (13 oz) can plum tomatoes

150 ml (¼ pint) fish stock or water

300 ml (½ pint) coconut milk

175 g (6 oz) raw tiger prawns, peeled

meat from 1 small cooked crab

salt and pepper

Sri Lankan spice mixture:

2 teaspoons coriander seeds

1 teaspoon cumin seeds

3 dried red chillies

1 teaspoon fennel seeds

¼ teaspoon fenugreek seeds

5 cm (2 inch) piece of cinnamon stick

½ teaspoon whole cloves

3 cardamom pods, seeds removed

1 teaspoon black peppercorns

1 teaspoon yellow mustard seeds

1 tablespoon basmati rice

Seafood curry is a great favourite of Sri Lankans. The spice mixture is a variation on Rani King and Chandra Khan's recipe. Any remainder can be kept in an airtight container, it should be used within 1 month for the freshest flavour.

1 First prepare the spice mixture. Spread all the spices on one baking sheet and the rice on a separate sheet and roast in a preheated oven, 200°C (400°F), Gas Mark 6, for 5–6 minutes or until toasted. The rice will take slightly longer than the spices. Stir occasionally to toast them evenly. Take care that the spices do not burn. Leave to cool then grind the spices and the toasted rice to a powder.

2 Rub 2 tablespoons of the spice mixture into the fish. Cover and set aside for 30 minutes to allow the flavours to mingle.

3 Heat 2 tablespoons of the oil in a saucepan and gently fry the onions for 20 minutes or until soft and golden brown. Add the garlic, bruised lemon grass, ginger, turmeric and curry leaves and cook for 2–3 minutes. Add the tomatoes, stock and coconut milk to the pan and simmer gently, stirring occasionally, for 15 minutes. Increase the heat and boil, stirring, for 10 minutes to thicken the sauce slightly. Season to taste with salt and pepper.

4 Heat the remaining oil in a frying pan and sear the fish on all sides. Add to the tomato sauce with the tiger prawns and crab meat and simmer gently for 6–7 minutes. Season to taste. Remove the pan from the heat and leave to stand, covered, for 8 minutes for the fish to finish cooking in the curry's residual heat before serving.

Serves 4

fish masala with coconut sambal

kan laut kelapa sambol, malaysia

4 small pomfret, mackerel, snapper or bream, gutted

1 teaspoon ground chilli

¼ teaspoon turmeric

½ teaspoon salt

4 tablespoons coconut or vegetable oil

Coconut sambal:

3 tablespoons boiling water

50 g (2 oz) desiccated coconut

½ teaspoon chilli powder

1 teaspoon ground fish powder or ground shrimp

3 curry leaves

1 piece of pandanus leaf (optional)

½ onion, finely chopped

1 teaspoon lemon juice

Coconut-fried fish with a spicy hot sambal is an everyday dish in Malaysia and India. The fish is rubbed with a spice mix then fried in coconut (palm) oil until crisp and golden brown.

1 Remove the scales from the fish, then fillet and chop them into 7 cm (3 inch) pieces. Mix the chilli, turmeric and salt and rub into the fish on all sides. Set aside for 1 hour to allow the flavours to develop.

2 To make the sambal, mix the boiling water into the desiccated coconut to moisten and set aside. Put all the remaining sambal ingredients into a blender and work to a smooth paste. Mix the paste into the moistened coconut then transfer to a small bowl.

3 Heat the oil until hot and fry the fish for 3 minutes on both sides until well cooked, golden brown and very crisp. Remove with a slotted spoon and drain on kitchen paper.

4 Serve the warm fish on banana leaves with the coconut sambal, plain boiled rice and lime pickle (optional). Eat with your fingers.

Serves 4

prawn patia

parsee patia, india

6 large dried red chillies, chopped

2 green chillies, chopped

1 teaspoon cumin seeds

1 teaspoon nigella (onion) seeds

6 garlic cloves, crushed

4 tablespoons vegetable oil

4 large onions, finely chopped

1 teaspoon ground coriander

1 teaspoon turmeric

1 teaspoon cayenne pepper

1 teaspoon garam masala

6 curry leaves

2 tablespoons tomato purée

300 ml (½ pint) Tamarind Water (see page 9)

5 cm (2 inch) piece of fresh root ginger, peeled and finely chopped

2 tablespoons chopped coriander

2 tablespoons soft brown sugar

1 kg (2 lb) raw king or tiger prawns, peeled

½ teaspoon salt

Prawn patia is a Parsee dish. Distinctively hot, sweet and sour, it has a thick, dark sauce made with jaggery (brown sugar), tamarind and fresh ginger.

1 Put the red and green chillies into a food processor with the cumin, nigella seeds and garlic and grind to a rough paste or pound with a pestle and mortar. Heat the oil in a large frying pan, add the spice paste and fry for 1–2 minutes then add the onions and fry, stirring frequently, for 8–10 minutes until golden.

2 Add the ground coriander, turmeric, cayenne pepper and garam masala and cook for 2 minutes, stirring constantly.

3 Add the curry leaves, tomato purée, tamarind water, ginger, coriander and sugar and simmer, uncovered, for 15 minutes or until the sauce is thick.

4 Add the prawns and salt and simmer for 5 minutes. Remove from the heat and leave to stand, covered, for 20 minutes to finish cooking in the residual heat. Plain basmati rice and a simple curried green vegetable would make a good accompaniment.

Serves 6

red duck curry with dates

xiangsu ya, china

2 duck breasts and 2 legs, chopped into 5 cm (2 inch) pieces

16 red dates, soaked in boiling water for 6 hours

50 g (2 oz) caster sugar

600 ml (1 pint) water

3 tablespoons soy sauce

125 ml (4 fl oz) Chinese red wine

4 shallots, finely chopped

2 garlic cloves, finely chopped

2.5 cm (1 inch) piece of fresh root ginger, peeled and finely chopped

½ teaspoon Chinese five spice powder

½ teaspoon Sichuan peppercorns

1 star anise

8 tablespoons plum sauce

2 teaspoons cornflour

50 g (2 oz) cashew nuts or gingko nuts, toasted

oil, for deep-frying

coriander sprigs, to garnish

Red duck with Chinese dates or plums is a traditional Chinese dish.

1 Heat the oil in a deep-fryer or large saucepan until hot enough to brown a cube of bread in 3 minutes. Add a few pieces of duck and deep-fry for 6–8 minutes or until crisp and golden brown. Remove with a slotted spoon and drain on kitchen paper. Repeat with the remaining duck.

2 Put the soaked dates in a pan with half of the sugar and 150 ml (¼ pint) of the water, bring to the boil. Simmer for 10 minutes or until the dates are plump.

3 Put the soy sauce, Chinese wine, shallots, garlic, ginger, five spice powder, peppercorns, star anise and plum sauce into the date pan with the remaining water and sugar. Bring to the boil and simmer for a further 20 minutes. Add the duck and simmer for 5 minutes.

4 Mix the cornflour with a little cold water and mix to a smooth paste. Stir the cornflour paste into the duck sauce and, stirring constantly, bring to the boil and cook until thickened. Add the toasted cashews and serve garnished with coriander sprigs.

Serves 4

seeds from 3 cardamom pods

¼ teaspoon cloves

¼ teaspoon ground nutmeg

½ teaspoon ground star anise

1 tablespoon ground coriander

½ teaspoon ground fenugreek

1 teaspoon chilli powder

½ teaspoon ground black pepper

250 g (8 oz) yellow dal, washed and soaked for 1 hour

600 ml (1 pint) water

4 tablespoons chopped coriander

2 large onions, chopped

125 g (4 oz) pumpkin, diced

150 g (5 oz) aubergine, diced

125 g (4 oz) potatoes, diced

4 tablespoons vegetable oil

1 teaspoon garam masala

750 g (1½ lb) chicken breasts, cubed

5 cm (2 inch) piece of fresh root ginger, peeled and grated

6 garlic cloves, crushed

4 tablespoons chopped fenugreek leaves

4 large tomatoes, chopped

4 large green chillies, finely chopped

2 teaspoons tomato purée

1 tablespoon dark brown sugar

150 ml (¼ pint) Tamarind Water (see page 9)

300 ml (½ pint) chicken stock

1 teaspoon white wine vinegar

juice of 1 lemon

salt and pepper

chicken dhansak

murgh dhansak, india

Dhansak is a meat, vegetable and lentil curry made with puréed lentils, aubergines, tomatoes and fenugreek leaves, but spinach can be substituted. A Parsee dish, it is eaten with Pulao Rice (see page 45) and often served at family meals.

1 Heat a dry frying pan until hot and add the cardamom, cloves and ground spices and dry-fry for 4–5 minutes or until the spices are toasted and releasing their aroma.

2 Put the dal into a saucepan with the water, 1 tablespoon of the chopped coriander, 2 teaspoons of the spice mixture, the onions, pumpkin, aubergine and potatoes. Simmer, covered, for 40 minutes or until the vegetables and lentils are very soft. Remove from the heat and purée to a smooth sauce.

3 Heat the oil and fry the remaining spice mixture with the garam masala. Add the chicken and fry on all sides to seal.

4 Add the ginger, garlic, the remaining chopped coriander, fenugreek leaves, tomatoes and green chillies to the pan and cook for 10 minutes.

5 Add the puréed dal mixture to the chicken with the tomato purée, sugar, tamarind water and stock. Simmer gently, covered, for 35 minutes or until the chicken has cooked through and is tender. Season to taste with salt and pepper and add the vinegar and lemon juice. Simmer for 5 minutes and serve.

Serves 4

green curry

gaeng khiaw wan, thailand

Hot, hot, hot. Thai curries have a thin sauce and are traditionally served from a communal bowl. Polite Thai table manners recommend adding only a tablespoon of food to a small mound of rice at any one time. South-east Asian aubergines are either the size of a pea and grow in clusters, or the size of a golf ball. Both types should only be cooked briefly to retain their crisp texture and preserve their green colour.

1 To make the green curry paste, place all the ingredients except the fish sauce and lime juice in a food processor and process to a semi-smooth paste. Add the fish sauce and lime juice and process to a smooth paste.

2 Heat the oil in a saucepan, add all of the green curry paste and fry for 2–3 minutes, stirring constantly. Add the coconut milk and water and bring to a fast simmer.

3 Add the chicken or other meat to the curry sauce and simmer gently for 8–10 minutes. Add the fish sauce, to taste, the aubergines, chopped coriander and lime leaves. Simmer for 5 minutes. Stir in the basil leaves just before serving.

Serves 4

2 tablespoons groundnut oil

300 ml (½ pint) coconut milk

150 ml (¼ pint) water

500 g (1 lb) chicken, beef, pork or duck, finely sliced

2–3 tablespoons fish sauce

150 g (5 oz) Thai green aubergines

1 tablespoon chopped coriander

3 lime leaves, shredded

20 holy basil leaves

Green curry paste:

3 tablespoons coriander leaves

4 coriander roots

4 shallots, chopped

3 green chillies, chopped

2 teaspoons coriander seeds

4 garlic cloves, crushed

1 teaspoon shrimp paste

2 lemon grass stalks, chopped

2.5 cm (1 inch) piece of fresh galangal, peeled and chopped

½ teaspoon white peppercorns

3 kaffir lime leaves, shredded

3 whole cloves

2 teaspoons caster sugar

2 tablespoons fish sauce

juice of 1 lime

---

3 tablespoons vegetable oil

8 chicken drumsticks

2 large onions, finely chopped

4 garlic cloves, crushed

5 cm (2 inch) piece of fresh root ginger, peeled and finely chopped

1 teaspoon ground cumin

1 teaspoon turmeric

1 teaspoon ground coriander

1 teaspoon cayenne pepper

6 tablespoons water

250 g (8 oz) tomatoes, roughly chopped

150 ml (¼ pint) thick Greek yogurt

2 tablespoons chopped coriander

1 tablespoon garam masala

½ teaspoon salt

juice of 1 lemon

boiled rice, to serve

simple gurkha chicken

umaleko kukhura, nepal

This is a version of a chicken dish regularly cooked by the Gurkha regiment at Sandhurst.

1 Heat the oil in a saucepan and fry the chicken drumsticks until the skin is crisp. Remove the chicken from the pan and keep warm. Add the onions, garlic and ginger to the pan and fry until the onions are soft and golden.

2 Reduce the heat and add the cumin, turmeric, ground coriander, cayenne and 1 tablespoon of the water and cook, stirring, for 2 minutes. Add the tomatoes, yogurt and half of the chopped coriander. Increase the heat, return the chicken to the pan with the remaining water and bring to the boil.

3 Sprinkle the garam masala over the chicken, cover and simmer gently for 20 minutes. Season to taste. Just before serving add the salt and lemon juice and the remaining chopped coriander. Serve with plenty of boiled rice to soak up the juices.

Serves 4

musaman curry

kaeng matsaman, thailand

A Thai curry is like a soup in consistency – watery but with plenty of flavour and chilli heat. This is one of the more mellow Thai curries, with plenty of galangal and turmeric to perfume the coconut sauce. Matsaman is the Thai word for Muslim, and this curry is so named because it comes from southern Thailand, where many of the Thai population are Muslim rather than Buddhist. The unused curry paste can be kept in the refrigerator for up to two weeks. Alternatively, divide it into tablespoon quantities and freeze.

1 First make the curry paste. Heat a dry wok or frying pan until hot. Add all the dried spices and toast lightly. Remove from the heat and blend in a food processor, with the shallots, coriander root, shrimp paste, garlic and lemon grass. Add the galangal, kaffir lime leaves and salt and blend to a fine paste. Alternatively, pound the ingredients to a paste using a pestle and mortar.

2 Heat the oil in a wok or heavy-based frying pan, add the garlic and fry for 1 minute or until softened and just turning golden brown. Add 2 tablespoons of the spice paste and, stirring constantly, fry for 2 minutes to cook the shallots.

3 Add the coconut milk and simmer gently to create a smooth sauce. Add the water and chicken and simmer for 5 minutes. Add the fish sauce and potato and simmer for 10–15 minutes or until the meat has cooked through and the potato is tender but crisp.

4 Add the onion, peanuts, sugar, kaffir lime leaves and tamarind water and simmer for 1 minute then serve garnished with red chilli.

Serves 4

---

2 tablespoons vegetable oil

2 garlic cloves, crushed

425 g (14 oz) can coconut milk

150 ml (¼ pint) water

500 g (1 lb) chicken or beef, diced

2 tablespoons fish sauce

1 large potato, roughly diced

1 onion, sliced lengthways

75 g (3 oz) roasted peanuts

1 tablespoon brown sugar

2 kaffir lime leaves, shredded

3 tablespoons Tamarind Water (see page 9)

red chilli, chopped, to garnish

Musaman curry paste:

6 large dried red chillies

1 tablespoon ground coriander

1 teaspoon ground cumin

2 teaspoons turmeric

1 teaspoon ground cinnamon

1 teaspoon ground cloves

1 teaspoon ground star anise

8 cardamom pods, bruised

4 shallots, chopped

1 teaspoon finely chopped coriander root

2 teaspoons shrimp paste

8 garlic cloves, crushed

5 cm (2 inch) piece of lemon grass stalk, chopped

2.5 cm (1 inch) piece of fresh galangal, peeled and chopped

4 kaffir lime leaves, shredded

1 teaspoon salt

stir-fries & searing

Frying and searing in hot oil is a popular means of cooking throughout Asia. Groundnut oil is a favourite in Thailand and Vietnam but in India, Indonesia and Malaysia, oil from the coconut is preferred. The wok is the most vital piece of kitchen equipment in China and through South-east Asia and Indonesia and used for dishes like Chinese Sichuan Scallops (see page 76) and Thai Chicken with Burnt Chilli Paste and Cashew Nuts (see page 81). In Japan and Korea cast-iron pots and frying pans are used for searing Tuna Teriyaki (see page 82) and Korean Beef (see page 79).

crisp fried fish with chilli & basil

pla phad pet kaprow, thailand

In the north-east of Thailand, along the banks of the Mekong River, riverside restaurants place their tables so that diners look out across the fast-moving water to Laos. It is from these waters that the highly prized catfish are caught. A dense and firm fleshed fish, it stands up to deep-frying and plenty of chilli. Catfish can be bought frozen in Thai stores and supermarkets in this country. Chop off the ugly-looking head and remove the fillet from the bone. Alternatively use sea bass or cod.

1 Blend the garlic, coriander roots, fresh and dried chillies and sugar in a food processor or pound to a paste using a pestle and mortar.

2 Heat 1 tablespoon of oil in a wok or frying pan and stir-fry the chilli paste sauce for about 1–2 minutes. Add the fish sauce, soy sauce and lime leaves and stir-fry for 1 minute then add the stock and bring to a fast boil. Continue boiling until the sauce has reduced a little.

3 Heat the oil for deep-frying in a saucepan and when it is hot add the pieces of fish and fry until crisp and golden brown. Remove the fish from the oil with a slotted spoon and add to the chilli paste sauce and toss together. Deep-fry the basil leaves for 30 seconds, remove and drain on kitchen paper.

4 Serve the fish topped with the deep-fried basil leaves and shreds of red chilli.

Serves 4

3 garlic cloves, thinly sliced

2 coriander roots, finely chopped

2 fresh red chillies, finely chopped

1 dried red chilli, finely chopped

3 teaspoons caster sugar

3 tablespoons fish sauce

3 tablespoons soy sauce

3 kaffir lime leaves, finely shredded

5 tablespoons fish stock or water

500 g (1 lb) catfish, sea bass or cod, filleted and cubed

oil, for deep-frying

To serve:

20–30 holy basil leaves

1 red chilli, shredded

fiery hot chilli prawns

udang sambal, indonesia

Udang sambal is a simple dish to prepare and is often cooked in Indonesia. Sour and chilli hot, these prawns are delicious with just plain boiled rice and a fried egg. I first saw this dish being cooked in northern Sumatra, in the depths of the jungle where, so far from the sea, they used dried prawns that had been soaked for 30 minutes in warm water. The sambal was pounded to a paste between a pebble and a rock, the family's pestle and mortar.

4 tablespoons vegetable oil

750 g (1½ lb) raw tiger prawns, peeled

2 tablespoons chopped coriander

boiled rice, to serve

Marinade:

1 tablespoon vegetable oil

3 garlic cloves, crushed

2 dried chillies, chopped

½ teaspoon coarsely ground black pepper

6 tablespoons Tamarind Water (see page 9)

2 teaspoons brown sugar

Sambal:

6 red chillies, chopped

4 garlic cloves, crushed

4 shallots, chopped

4 tomatoes, chopped

1 teaspoon shrimp paste (*terasi*)

1 tablespoon small dried prawns (optional)

1 To make the marinade, heat the oil and fry the garlic and chillies for 1 minute. Add the black pepper, tamarind water and sugar and bring to the boil. Remove from the heat and allow to cool completely. Pour over the raw prawns, cover and leave to marinate in the refrigerator for 2–3 hours.

2 Put all the ingredients for the sambal into a food processor and blend to a paste or use a pestle and mortar. Heat 2 tablespoons of the oil in a frying pan and fry the paste, stirring constantly, for 3–4 minutes, to cook the shallots and reduce the paste to a thick chutney.

3 Heat the remaining oil in a wok or frying pan and add the prawns but not the marinade and stir-fry for 2–3 minutes or until the prawns are cooked through. Then add the marinade to the wok and, stirring constantly, fry the prawns in the sauce for 1 minute. Stir in the chopped coriander. Serve with boiled rice and the warm sambal.

Serves 4

tofu & beansprouts in peanut sauce

tahu goreng, malaysia

6 tablespoons vegetable oil

250 g (8 oz) firm tofu, cut into thick squares

3 garlic cloves, crushed

175 g (6 oz) bean sprouts

50 g (2 oz) pak choi, roughly chopped

75 g (3 oz) roasted peanuts, chopped

2 tablespoons light soy sauce

150 ml (¼ pint) coconut milk

2 red chillies, chopped

salt and pepper

handful of coriander leaves, to serve

Tofu (tahu) is available in soft and firm versions. Use firm tofu for stir-frying and remember that it soaks up oil like a sponge, so keep the oil hot and sear the surface of the tofu quickly. Tofu absorbs strongly flavoured ingredients like this Malaysian peanut and coconut sauce and will hold together well during braising and stir-frying.

1 Heat the oil in a wok and fry the tofu until crisp and golden brown on the outside. Remove from the oil and drain on kitchen paper. Reserve.

2 Add the garlic, bean sprouts, pak choi and peanuts to the oil and stir-fry for about 2–3 minutes or until the vegetables begin to wilt. Add the soy sauce and coconut milk and toss together. Simmer for a further 2 minutes.

3 Just before serving add the chopped chillies, salt, pepper and the pieces of fried tofu. Carefully toss together and serve topped with coriander leaves.

Serves 4

2 tablespoons oil

750 g (1½ lb) scallops

2 garlic cloves, crushed

1 dried red chilli, finely chopped

½ teaspoon Chinese five spice powder

2.5 cm (1 inch) piece of fresh root ginger, peeled and finely shredded

2 tablespoons Chinese wine

2 tablespoons dark soy sauce

3 tablespoons water

6 spring onions, diagonally sliced

1 small onion, sliced

1 teaspoon caster sugar

2 spring onions, shredded, to garnish

sichuan scallops

qingchao baoyu, west china

Food from the region of Sichuan, in west China, is hot and spicy. Chilli, ginger, onion and garlic are used liberally and are in great evidence in this fiery scallop dish. The scallop is a very tender piece of seafood and needs only to be shown to the heat of the wok, for an instant, in order to sear the outside. Never overcook.

1 Heat the oil in a wok or heavy-based frying pan until smoking hot. Add the scallops and sear on both sides, remove and reserve.

2 Add the garlic, chilli, Chinese five spice powder and ginger and stir-fry for 1 minute. Add the Chinese wine, soy sauce, water, spring onions, onion and caster sugar and stir-fry for 1 minute then return the scallops to the wok and stir-fry them in the sauce for no longer than 2 minutes or they will become tough.

3 Arrange the scallops with their sauce on a warmed serving dish and garnish with the spring onions.

Serves 4

pork with ginger & shiitake mushrooms

jiangbao rouding, singapore

Singaporean cuisine is predominantly Chinese, with the small Arabic and Indian communities adding their cultural influences. Not surprisingly, it is the Chinese who dominate the food markets and restaurants. Straits Chinese, as they are called, have adapted some of their original styles of cooking none more so, than the Nonya community who are an equal mix of Chinese and Malay people. This Chinese stir-fry has a Malaysian twist.

2 tablespoons groundnut or vegetable oil

2 garlic cloves, finely chopped

10 cm (4 inch) piece of fresh root ginger, peeled and shredded

500 g (1 lb) pork fillet, finely shredded

6 tablespoons dark soy sauce

4 tablespoons Chinese rice wine

125 g (4 oz) shiitake mushrooms, thickly sliced or 25 g (1 oz) dried black fungus, soaked and roughly chopped

½ teaspoon sugar

1 green chilli, shredded

1 small onion, sliced

1 teaspoon cornflour, mixed to a thin paste with 1 tablespoon water

4 spring onions, diagonally sliced

To serve:

chilli oil

4 tablespoons finely chopped roasted peanuts

handful of coriander leaves

1 Heat the oil in a wok or heavy-based frying pan, add the garlic and ginger and fry until golden brown.

2 Add the pork and stir-fry for 1 minute. Add the soy sauce and Chinese wine and stir-fry for 1 further minute. Add the mushrooms, sugar, green chilli, onion and cornflour paste and stir-fry briskly for 1 minute or until the sauce has thickened slightly.

3 Just before serving add the sliced spring onions and stir once. Remove from the heat and serve the pork with chilli oil, roasted peanuts and coriander leaves.

Serves 4

korean beef with fiery hot cabbage

songyee basut boekum, korea

500 g (1 lb) sirloin beef

1 egg, beaten

2 teaspoons cornflour

2 tablespoons vegetable oil

2 garlic cloves, crushed

½ teaspoon salt

125 g (4 oz) dried shiitake mushrooms, soaked in warm water for 30 minutes

1 teaspoon caster sugar

6 spring onions, diagonally sliced

2 red chillies, finely sliced

125 g (4 oz) kimchi

1 tablespoon toasted white or black sesame seeds

boiled rice, to serve

A meal wouldn't be complete in Korea if kimchi, the nation's favourite dish, wasn't used. A fermented pickle of Chinese cabbage in a chilli and garlic vinegar base, it has a powerful flavour and is used or served as a vegetable rather than a pickle. Many Korean households make their own, using old family recipes, but it can be bought in oriental stores.

1 Half freeze the beef until firm and then with a sharp knife slice it very thinly. Place the beef slices in a bowl, add the egg and sift the cornflour over the top. Leave to stand for 10 minutes.

2 Heat the oil in a wok or large frying pan, add the beef and fry for 1 minute, stirring constantly, then add the garlic and salt. Stir-fry for 1 extra minute.

3 Thickly slice the shiitake mushrooms and add to the wok with the sugar, spring onions and chillies and stir-fry for 1 further minute. Add the kimchi and the sesame seeds and toss together. Serve with boiled rice.

Serves 4

chicken with burnt chilli paste & cashew nuts

gai nam prik pow met ma muang, thailand

3 tablespoons groundnut oil or vegetable oil

2 garlic cloves, thinly sliced

375 g (12 oz) chicken breasts, skinned and cubed

2 tablespoons fish sauce

2 tablespoons water

2 teaspoons sugar

1 red chilli, sliced

10 holy or sweet basil leaves

4 kaffir lime leaves, shredded

125 g (4 oz) roasted cashew nuts

Burnt chilli paste (*nam prik pow*):

3 tablespoons groundnut oil

1 small red onion, finely chopped

6–8 large dried red chillies, finely chopped

6 garlic cloves, finely chopped

1 tablespoon dried prawns (optional)

2 tablespoons fish sauce

1 tablespoon Tamarind Water (see page 9)

2 tablespoons brown sugar

To garnish:

1 red chilli, sliced

basil sprigs

Burnt chilli paste (nam prik pow) is a classic Thai spice paste which is used in many stir-fry dishes and added to soups for extra flavour and colour. Make it from scratch and store in the refrigerator for up to 3–4 weeks or buy it ready-made from oriental stores.

1 First make the burnt chilli paste. Heat the oil, add the onion and fry until softened. Remove with a slotted spoon and reserve. Add the chillies and fry until blackened, remove and reserve. Add the garlic and fry until golden brown.

2 Grind the prawns, if using, add half of the fried chillies and blend coarsely. Add the onion and garlic and blend to a coarse paste. Add the mixture to the oil with the fish sauce, tamarind water and sugar. Heat gently for 2–3 minutes, stirring constantly.

3 Heat the oil in a wok or heavy-based frying pan and fry the sliced garlic until beginning to brown. Add the chicken and fry quickly on all sides. Crumble the remaining fried chillies over the chicken and add 2 tablespoons of the chilli paste, the fish sauce, water, sugar and chilli to the pan. Stir-fry over a high heat. Add the basil leaves, kaffir lime leaves and cashew nuts and stir-fry for 1 more minute. Garnish with sliced red chilli and basil sprigs.

Serves 4

750 g (1½ lb) very fresh tuna, cut into 5 cm (2 inch) squares or rectangles

½ teaspoon salt

2 tablespoons vegetable oil

Teriyaki sauce:

4 tablespoons sake

4 tablespoons mirin

4 tablespoons dark soy sauce

2 teaspoons caster sugar

2 teaspoons Ginger Juice (see page 8)

To serve:

12 asparagus spears, blanched

pickled ginger

tuna teriyaki

bonito teriyaki, japan

Fish or beef teriyaki cooks to a wonderful golden red crust and is slightly crispy on the outside and deliciously juicy on the inside. For this recipe make sure the tuna is as fresh as possible and do not overcook. Heating the pan until it is very hot is vital for sealing in the juices and creating a golden crust.

1 First make the teriyaki sauce. Put the sake, mirin, soy sauce and caster sugar in a small saucepan and bring to the boil. Remove from the heat and leave to cool. Stir in the ginger juice.

2 Rub both sides of the fish with salt to firm it. Set aside for 30 minutes, then rinse off the salt and put the fish pieces in the teriyaki sauce and leave to marinate for 1 hour.

3 Heat the oil in a pan until smoking hot. Remove the tuna from the marinade and add to the hot pan. Sear the surface, turn the tuna over and sear the second side and cook for 1 further minute. Pour the teriyaki sauce over the fish and cook for 1 more minute.

4 Remove the fish from the pan and serve with the asparagus spears. Allow the sauce to bubble and thicken and then spoon a little over each of the pieces of fish and serve with a mound of pickled ginger.

Serves 4

grilling & roasting

Cooking over open coals evokes a delightful scene and, in Vietnam, Barbecue Beef Wrapped in Rice Paper (see page 94) arrives at the table with a small tabletop barbecue so that it can be cooked to order. Thai Barbecued Chicken (see page 91) and Vietnamese Sizzling Fish in Banana Leaves (see page 86) are dishes typically found in outdoor markets cooked over the coals. India and China have the most developed cuisines in Asia and have been roasting for centuries. The classic Peking Duck (see page 93) is always popular but equally as good is Indian spiced Raan of Lamb (see page 97) and Sri Lankan Beef (see page 89).

sizzling fish in banana leaves

ca roti, vietnam

4 large squares of banana leaf

4 x 175 g (6 oz) swordfish, snapper or sea bass fillets, 2.5 cm (1 inch) thick

salt and pepper

Spice paste:

1 lemon grass stalk, very finely chopped

2 large garlic cloves, finely chopped

1 kaffir lime leaf, finely shredded

2 shallots, finely chopped

125 g (4 oz) butter

2 teaspoons lime juice

1 tablespoon finely chopped coriander leaves

1 green chilli, finely chopped

1 red chilli, finely chopped

To serve:

boiled rice

stir-fried green vegetable

On Hoi An's waterfront, in central Vietnam, is Restaurant du Port. Run by a local family, the two young sisters front the restaurant while at the back their mother runs the kitchen like clockwork, with their brothers and other relatives serving guests and toing and froing with supplies. This is one of their specialities – a sizzling dish of aromatic fish wrapped in banana leaves and cooked over coals. It can also be made with large king prawns or chicken fillets.

1 First make the spice paste. Blend the lemon grass, garlic, kaffir lime leaf and shallots to a smooth paste in a food processor or with a pestle and mortar. Add the butter, lime juice, coriander, green and red chillies, salt and pepper to taste and blend again.

2 Put the banana leaves into a bowl and pour boiling water over them, then drain; this makes them easier to bend and wrap. Place a fish fillet in the centre of each leaf and cover it with some of the lemon grass mixture. Wrap it up tightly and secure with a bamboo skewer or cocktail stick.

3 Chill the fish parcels in the refrigerator until needed or put them on a preheated barbecue and cook for 8–10 minutes, turning once. Serve wrapped in the banana leaves. Cut open the parcel and the aromatic, buttery fish awaits. Eat with boiled rice and a stir-fried green vegetable.

Serves 4

garlic clams

con nghieu roti, vietnam

1 kg (2 lb) large clams

125 g (4 oz) butter, plus extra
for serving

3 garlic cloves, crushed

1 lemon grass stalk, bruised

juice of 2 limes

½ teaspoon salt

½ teaspoon pepper

During February and May; charcoal cooked clams are a Hoi An speciality. East of the town is the endless stretch of Cua Dai beach, where local families from the fishing village moonlight and run palm-fringed shaded areas where they cook fish (ca), prawns (tom), squid (muk) and these large clams (con nghieu) over charcoal. These are best eaten with freshly cooked frites, which are also dipped into the seasoned lime juice. To eat, pour a little lime juice over each clam and scoop into the mouth, like eating an oyster. They are smoky flavoured and simply delicious.

1 Wash the clams and discard any that are open. Mix the butter with the garlic and ½ tablespoon finely chopped lemon grass. Heat gently to melt the butter while stirring it with the remaining part of the stalk of bruised lemon grass.

2 Lay the clams on a rack over a preheated barbecue and cook until they open. Brush liberally with the melted butter using the bruised lemon grass stalk.

3 Cook for 3–4 minutes then serve immediately with a little extra butter brushed over the clams. Mix the lime juice with the salt and pepper and serve as a dip.

Serves 4

sri lankan beef

smoore, sri lanka

1.5 kg (3 lb) piece stewing beef

2 onions, chopped

5 garlic cloves

1 tablespoon finely chopped fresh root ginger

1 cinnamon stick

2 cloves

2 star anise

12 curry leaves

1 lemon grass stalk

2 tablespoons malt vinegar

1 tablespoon chilli powder

2 teaspoons ground turmeric

1 tablespoon ground cumin

2 teaspoons ground mixed spice

2 teaspoons salt

2 teaspoons pepper

juice of 3 lemons

1 teaspoon brown sugar

200 g (7 oz) block creamed coconut, roughly chopped

3 tablespoons ghee or coconut oil

Sambal:

1 red onion, finely chopped

4 tomatoes, finely chopped

2 tablespoons chopped coriander leaves

To serve:

Rice with Raisins and Cashews (see page 45)

Pumpkin and Sweet Onions (see page 120)

This recipe belongs to Rani King and Chandra Khan. Their father was a Sri Lankan diplomat and as children they lived in Sri Lanka and learnt about the delicious spicy dishes found there. Their experiences have resulted in their successful company selling authentic spice mixes and relishes. This is one of my favourite recipes, it is fragrant and the meat is succulent, perfect for Sunday lunch.

1 Using a sharp knife, stab the meat all over. Put all the ingredients, except the creamed coconut and ghee, into a large saucepan with a lid. Simmer over a moderate heat for 1–1½ hours or until the meat is tender. Add extra water if needed to stop the beef sticking.

2 Add the creamed coconut, and cook, uncovered, over a high heat for 10 minutes. Keep turning the meat and stirring the sauce to prevent it from catching. The sauce will have reduced to a thick consistency.

3 To make the sambal, combine all the ingredients in a bowl and mix thoroughly. Cover and chill until ready to serve.

4 Remove the meat from the pan. Heat the ghee or oil in a frying pan until hot, add the meat and sear on all sides. Pour the sauce over the beef and simmer for 5–6 minutes to heat the sauce through. Serve the beef in thick slices with Rice with Raisins and Cashews, Pumpkin and Sweet Onions and the sambal.

Serves 4

thai barbecued chicken

gai yaang, thailand

In most Thai towns there is an evening market where all the locals congregate and have supper or buy items to take home to include in their family meal. This spatchcocked chicken is cooked gently over charcoal until tender and crisp and served with a dipping sauce and sticky rice. Chicken portions can be used instead but only cook them for 10–15 minutes.

1 Rub the chicken all over with salt and pepper and place in a shallow container.

2 Put the galangal, garlic, red chilli, shallots and coriander in a food processor and blend to a paste or use a pestle and mortar. Add the coconut milk and mix until well blended.

3 Pour this coconut marinade over the chicken, cover and leave to marinate overnight in the refrigerator.

4 Remove the chicken from the marinade, place it on a hot barbecue and cook for 30–40 minutes for spatchcocked chicken and 10–15 minutes for the chicken breasts, turning and basting regularly with the remaining marinade. The whole chicken is cooked when a skewer inserted in one of the legs reveals clear juices.

5 Leave the chicken to stand for 5 minutes then chop it into small pieces with a cleaver. Serve with the dipping sauce, sticky rice and lime wedges. Garnish with chive flowers and eat with fingers.

Serves 4–6

1.5 kg (3 lb) chicken, spatchcocked, or part-boned chicken breasts

5 cm (2 inch) piece of fresh galangal, peeled and finely chopped

4 garlic cloves, crushed

1 large red chilli, finely chopped

4 shallots, finely chopped

2 tablespoons finely chopped coriander leaves

150 ml (¼ pint) thick coconut milk

salt and pepper

To serve:

1 quantity Sweet Chilli Sauce (see page 141)

Sticky Rice (see page 45)

lime wedges

250 g (8 oz) boneless, skinless chicken, cubed

3 tablespoons oyster sauce

2 tablespoons water

1 tablespoon soy sauce

2 teaspoons sesame oil

2 garlic cloves, crushed

2 tablespoons rice flour

bunch of pandanus leaves, blanched

Dipping sauce:

4 tablespoons rice vinegar

1 tablespoon caster sugar

1 green bird chilli, finely chopped

1 red bird chilli, finely chopped

2.5 cm (1 inch) cucumber, finely diced

chicken wrapped in pandanus leaves

gai hoh bai teoy, thailand

These little morsels of chicken are wrapped in blanched pandanus (screwpine) leaves and barbecued until succulent and cooked through. They can also be slowly deep-fried. Wrap in blanched banana leaves or aluminium foil if pandanus leaves are hard to find in oriental stores.

1 Place the cubed chicken in a bowl. Mix together the oyster sauce, water, soy sauce, sesame oil, garlic and flour and pour over the chicken. Coat well in the marinade, cover and leave overnight to allow the flavours to develop.

2 Holding 2 pandanus leaves overlapping at an angle to each other, fold 1 over the other twice and then slip 1 length of leaf under a fold to create a knot. Place a piece of chicken on the fold, wrap the leaves in a tight parcel and secure with a wooden cocktail stick.

3 Place all the ingredients for the sauce, except the cucumber, in a small saucepan and heat gently until the sugar has dissolved. Remove from the heat and leave to cool then add the cucumber.

4 Place the chicken parcels on to a hot barbecue and cook turning frequently for 10–12 minutes, or until the leaves are well charred. Remove one of the chicken parcels and look inside to check that the chicken has cooked through. Serve while still warm, with the dipping sauce.

Serves 4

peking duck

beijing kaoya, china

2 kg (4 lb) oven-ready duck

Marinade:

1 tablespoon hoisin sauce

150 ml (¼ pint) Chinese rice wine

3 tablespoons brown sugar

4 tablespoons honey

4 tablespoons soy sauce

2 teaspoons Ginger Juice
(see page 8)

2–3 drops red food colouring
(optional)

150 ml (¼ pint) water

To serve:

24 ready-made Chinese pancakes

½ cucumber, finely shredded

8 spring onions, finely shredded

6–8 tablespoons hoisin or
plum sauce

Peking duck is one of the favourite choices in Chinese restaurants: cooked until crisp, the flesh and skin are wrapped in wheat pancakes with hoisin sauce, shredded spring onions and cucumber. In a restaurant Peking duck goes through a lengthy preparation process. First the skin is forced away from the flesh by pumping air between the two, then it is dipped in a spiced malt sugar solution, dried for hours and cooked hanging in a tandoori-style oven. Of course this isn't possible in the domestic kitchen, but this recipe is a good home version. Hanging the duck to dry is vital to the end result, so it is well worth buying a duck hook from an oriental store. Alternatively, use a butcher's hook. Using a fan to blow cold air on the duck will help the drying process.

1 Prick the duck all over with a fork, put it in a bowl and pour boiling water over it. Hang it up until dry.

2 Place the hoisin sauce, rice wine, brown sugar, honey, soy sauce, ginger juice, red food colouring, if using, and water in a wide saucepan and stir until dissolved. Bring to the boil and boil until it forms a thick syrup.

3 Loop a string or metal skewer through the neck cavity and, holding the duck over the simmering marinade, spoon the mixture over the duck several times. Hang up the duck in a cool place and leave overnight to dry.

4 Place the duck, breast side down, on a rack in a baking tin and roast in a preheated oven, 240°C (475°F), Gas Mark 9, for 15 minutes. Reduce the heat to 190°C (375°F), Gas Mark 5 and roast for 1½ hours, turning twice during cooking. Cover the duck with foil if it begins to over-brown.

5 Remove the duck from the oven to a warmed serving dish and leave to stand for 15 minutes. Steam the pancakes for about 5 minutes, then carve the duck into thin slices and shred. Serve with the steamed pancakes, shredded cucumber, spring onions and hoisin or plum sauce.

Serves 4

barbecued beef wrapped in rice paper

thit bo nuong ra, vietnam

500 g (1 lb) fillet of beef

1 lemon grass stalk, very finely chopped

1 garlic clove, crushed

2 teaspoons fish sauce

Nuoc mam dipping sauce:

6 tablespoons fish sauce

2 teaspoons caster sugar

1 tablespoon rice vinegar

3 red bird chillies, finely chopped

2 green bird chillies, finely chopped

To serve:

32 medium rice papers

2 tablespoons toasted sesame seeds

handful of mint sprigs

1 red chilli, chopped

This Vietnamese speciality is at its best when it is cooked over a small coal barbecue. In a restaurant, the barbecue is brought to your table with a plate of dry-marinated sliced beef and a second plate of rice papers, assorted lettuce leaves and mint leaves. The beef is cooked to order, then you wrap it in the rice paper like a cigar and pop it in your mouth.

1 Put the beef in the freezer for 30 minutes–1 hour so that it is firm but not frozen. Using a sharp knife, cut the fillet across the grain into thin slices. Make the dipping sauce: mix together all the ingredients and leave to stand for 1 hour.

2 Arrange the beef on 4 individual serving plates. Sprinkle it with the lemon grass, garlic and fish sauce and set aside for 30 minutes before serving.

3 Dip the sheets of rice paper briefly in water to moisten. Divide them between 4 smaller plates with the sprigs of mint and set out individual bowls of dipping sauce.

4 Light a small barbecue or heat a table-top cooker and give a plate of beef and plate of rice papers to each person. The beef is cooked by each person according to how rare or well done they prefer their meat (1 minute for rare and 3–4 minutes for well done). To eat, place a slice of beef on a rice paper, sprinkle it with toasted sesame seeds and a few mint leaves and wrap it up like a cigar and sprinkle with chopped chilli. Dip the wrapped-up beef into the dipping sauce before eating.

Serves 4

chinese five spice
spare ribs

paigu ganshao, china

Sticky, finger-licking spare ribs are a Chinese favourite and are always included at a banquet. Coated in a hoisin-based marinade and simmered until tender and glazed, they are excellent as an appetizer served with young Cos or romaine lettuce leaves, with Spring Rolls (see page 32).

1 Separate the ribs into individual pieces and, using a cleaver, chop them into 7.5 cm (3 inch) lengths or ask your butcher to do this for you.

2 Heat the oil in a deep-fryer or large saucepan until a cube of bread browns in 3 minutes. Add the spare rib pieces and deep-fry for 6–8 minutes or until golden brown and crisp. Remove with a slotted spoon and drain on kitchen paper.

3 Place the chicken stock, Chinese five spice powder, sugar, hoisin or plum sauce, yellow bean sauce, rice wine, garlic, ginger, shallots and soy sauce in a saucepan and heat gently to dissolve the sugar. Mix the cornflour with a little water and stir it into the sauce. Bring to the boil and boil until thickened. Reduce the heat, add the spare ribs and simmer gently, uncovered, for 45 minutes or until tender.

4 Spread the ribs on a rack, standing on a baking sheet, and brush with plenty of the sauce. Roast in a preheated oven, 200°C (400°F), Gas Mark 6, for 15 minutes or until piping hot and browning slightly.

Serves 4

750 g (1½ lb) spare ribs

600 ml (1 pint) chicken stock

½ teaspoon Chinese five spice powder

½ tablespoon caster sugar

4 tablespoons hoisin or plum sauce

2 teaspoons yellow bean sauce

4 tablespoons Chinese rice wine

3 garlic cloves, crushed

2.5 cm (1 inch) piece of fresh root ginger, finely chopped

2 shallots, finely chopped

2 tablespoons dark soy sauce

1 tablespoon cornflour

groundnut or vegetable oil, for deep-frying

raan of lamb

kashmiri raan, india & pakistan

A raan is first marinated in a mixture of yogurt, almonds and saffron and then slowly roasted until tender. It makes a spectacular centrepiece for a special occasion and is sometimes decorated with silver leaf. I first tasted it at a family lunch in Delhi. On this occasion it was a raan of venison; thinly sliced, it was magnificent, with an array of vegetables and home-made pickles. This recipe comes from Geeta Samtani.

1 Trim the leg of lamb of all the fat and, using a sharp knife, make a series of cuts in the meat.

2 Combine the ginger, garlic, spices, lemon juice and oil and rub the mixture all over the lamb.

3 Mix together the yogurt, ground almonds, pistachios, saffron and its liquid and honey to make a smooth marinade, season to taste with salt and pepper and spread over the leg of lamb. Leave the lamb to marinate overnight or up to 2 days in the refrigerator.

4 Put the lamb in a roasting tin with the marinade and roast in the centre of a preheated oven, 230°C (450°F), Gas Mark 8, for 30 minutes. Reduce the heat to 190°C (375°F), Gas Mark 5 and roast the lamb for a further 1¾ hours.

5 Remove the leg of lamb from the oven, loosely cover with foil and leave to stand for 10 minutes. Sprinkle the lamb with toasted blanched almonds, then slice it and serve with a good mango chutney.

Serves 6–8

2.5 kg (5 lb) leg of lamb

2 tablespoons finely chopped fresh root ginger

6 garlic cloves, crushed

1 teaspoon ground cumin

1 teaspoon turmeric

1 teaspoon ground black pepper

½ teaspoon ground cinnamon

1 teaspoon ground cardamom

½ teaspoon ground cloves

2 tablespoons lemon juice

2 tablespoons vegetable oil

250 ml (8 fl oz) thick yogurt

50 g (2 oz) ground almonds

50 g (2 oz) pistachio nuts, roughly chopped

½ teaspoon saffron, soaked in 2 tablespoons hot water

1 tablespoon clear honey

salt and pepper

50 g (2 oz) toasted blanched almonds

mango chutney, to serve

steaming & one-pot

Steaming and poaching are techniques frequently used in China and Japan. Steaming is an ideal method for making light dishes like Thai Curried Fish in Banana Leaves (see page 103) and Drunken Chicken (see page 106). In Thailand, Vietnam, Cambodia and Laos, dishes like Beef Cooked in Vinegar (see page 111) and Fish Hotpot (see page 101) are cooked in large charcoal-fuelled pots filled with a poaching liquid. These pots are known as steamboats and are brought to the table once the food has been cooked. Slow braised dishes like Braised Pigeons with Dried Plums (see page 107) and Aromatic Braised Duck (see page 108) are traditional aromatic dishes using dried fruits and spices to great effect. The long slow cooking develops those flavours.

fish hotpot

lau ca, cambodia

Cambodian cooking borrows extensively from Vietnamese and Thai cooking; this lau, *using seafood or chicken, can be found in both those countries. The seafood or meat is gently poached in a mixture of stock and coconut water. Coconut water comes from a green coconut or it can be bought in small tins in oriental stores as a ready-prepared drink. This is not coconut milk, which is made from the flesh of the coconut, but the liquid found at the centre of the coconut. If you are using a fresh coconut, make three holes at the top with a corkscrew and pour out the water.*

1 Heat the sesame and vegetable oils together, add the shallots and garlic and fry gently for 2 minutes or until softened but not browned.

2 Add the onion, coconut water, rice wine vinegar, lemon grass, lime leaves, chillies, stock and sugar to the pan, bring to the boil and boil for 2 minutes. Reduce the heat and add the tomatoes, fish sauce and tomato purée and cook for 5 minutes.

3 Blanch the rice noodles in boiling water for 1 minute. Drain and refresh in cold water. Divide between 4 serving bowls.

4 Just before serving add the prawns, squid rings, clams and mushrooms to the hotpot and simmer gently for 5–6 minutes or until the seafood is cooked. Stir in the basil leaves.

5 Serve the hotpot immediately with the rice noodles. Each diner ladles stock on to their noodles and seafood then adds dipping sauce, to taste, and coriander leaves.

Serves 4

1 teaspoon sesame oil

1 tablespoon vegetable oil

3 shallots, chopped

3 garlic cloves, crushed

1 sweet onion, halved and sliced

600 ml (1 pint) coconut water

3 tablespoons rice wine vinegar

1 lemon grass stalk, chopped

4 kaffir lime leaves

6 red bird chillies

300 ml (½ pint) fish stock or water

1 tablespoon caster sugar

2 tomatoes, quartered

4 tablespoons fish sauce

1 teaspoon tomato purée

375 g (12 oz) fresh rice noodles (see page 9)

375 g (12 oz) tiger prawns, heads removed and peeled

125 g (4 oz) squid, cleaned and cut into rings

175 g (6 oz) clams, scrubbed

400 g (13 oz) can straw mushrooms, drained

20 holy basil leaves

To serve:

1 quantity Nuoc Mam Dipping Sauce (see page 94)

handful of coriander leaves

tofu & fish hotpot

oden, japan

6 Chinese cabbage leaves

125 g (4 oz) sugar snap peas

300 g (10 oz) cellophane noodles (*saifan*)

2 boneless, skinless chicken thighs

125 g (4 oz) sea bream fillets

125 g (4 oz) mackerel fillets

1.8 litres (3 pints) fish stock

5 tablespoons mirin

2.5 cm (1 inch) piece of fresh root ginger, peeled and grated

6 spring onions, chopped

1 tablespoon soy sauce

175 g (6 oz) clams

125 g (4 oz) small cooked prawns, shelled

250 g (8 oz) firm tofu, cubed

75 g (3 oz) watercress, chopped

125 g (4 oz) enoki or shiitake mushroooms, halved

Red maple relish:

75 g (3 oz) daikon

2 small chillies

One-pot cooking is popular in Japan. It allows all the diners to get involved in the cooking. Very simple to prepare, this dish is often referred to as a wrestler's hotpot because of the variety and quantity of protein it contains. The red maple relish made with grated daikon (white radish) and chilli is a traditional accompaniment. It should be very finely grated, almost to a purée.

1 Blanch the cabbage and sugar snap peas in boiling water for 1 minute, then drain and refresh in cold water. Shred the cabbage.

2 Place the noodles in a large bowl, cover with hot water and leave to soak for about 10 minutes or until softened.

3 Slice the chicken into cubes and the fish into 5 cm (2 inch) pieces. Put the stock, mirin, ginger, spring onions and soy sauce into a large pan and bring to the boil. Reduce the heat to a simmer, add the chicken and simmer for 8–10 minutes.

4 To make the red maple relish, make two deep holes in the large end of the daikon with a chopstick and insert the chillies. Grate the daikon and chillies together very finely. Then put them in a mortar and pound with a pestle.

5 Add the clams, prawns, sliced fish, soaked noodles and tofu to the simmering hotpot and take it to the table. Simmer for a further 6–8 minutes or until the clams open and the fish has cooked. Discard any clams that remain closed.

6 Arrange the cabbage, blanched sugar snaps, watercress, mushrooms and red maple relish on a serving platter and serve with the hotpot. Add the mushrooms and watercress to the hotpot and cook for 1 minute. Place a few items in each serving bowl and ladle some stock over the top. Allow diners to help themselves to more as they eat.

Serves 6

curried fish in banana leaves

haw muk, thailand

12 x 15 cm (6 inch) diameter circles of banana leaf

500 g (1 lb) white fish, chopped

3 tablespoons Thai Red Curry Paste (see page 8)

2 tablespoons desiccated coconut

1 tablespoon chopped coriander leaves

1 tablespoon ground roasted peanuts

2 kaffir lime leaves, finely shredded

2 eggs, beaten

1 tablespoon fish sauce

50 g (2 oz) Chinese cabbage, shredded

1 large red chilli, chopped

1 large green chilli, chopped

300 ml (½ pint) coconut milk

salt and pepper

These banana leaf cups of steamed fish are very popular in Bangkok. Roadside stalls and evening markets sell them fresh from large steamers. The cups are slightly square and are made by stapling the pleats of the leaf cup. If banana leaves are difficult to find use small tea cups or bowls.

1 To make the banana leaf bowls, place 2 rounds of banana leaf together, pleat at opposite sides and staple.

2 Put the fish, red curry paste, coconut, coriander, peanuts, lime leaves and eggs in a food processor with the fish sauce. Season with salt and pepper and blend until smooth.

3 Divide the Chinese cabbage between the banana cups and spoon the fish mixture over the top. Arrange the red and green chillies on the cabbage and divide the coconut milk between the cups. Put the banana cups in a steamer and steam over boiling water for 20 minutes or until set.

Serves 6

hainanese chicken with ginger pickle

hainan jitui fan, singapore

2 kg (4 lb) corn-fed chicken, jointed

7 cm (3 inch) piece of fresh root ginger, peeled and grated

1.8 litres (3 pints) water

1 onion, chopped

1 teaspoon salt

3 teaspoons sesame oil

Ginger pickle:

175 g (6 oz) fresh root ginger, peeled and grated

1 red chilli, chopped

1 large garlic clove, crushed

1 tablespoon caster sugar

1 teaspoon salt

250 ml (8 fl oz) rice wine vinegar

Rice:

375 g (12 oz) long-grain rice

1 tablespoon vegetable oil

2 garlic cloves, crushed

½ teaspoon salt

¼ teaspoon pepper

To serve:

1 small cucumber, thickly sliced

2 spring onions

1 red chilli, deseeded and finely chopped (optional)

2 tablespoons coriander leaves

2 spring onions, chopped

Hainanese chicken restaurants and char siu bun *teashops are popular places in Singapore to lunch and have breakfast. Many of the local Hainanese eateries sell this lunchtime speciality. The office workers race in for a plate of steaming rice, topped with poached chicken and a ginger dipping sauce, accompanied by a bowl of chicken soup and a glass of chilled green tea. The ginger pickle is vital to the dish and is found on each formica-topped table in a plain jam jar.*

1 First make the ginger pickle. Place the ginger, chilli, garlic, sugar and salt in a food processor and blend to a rough purée, or use a pestle and mortar. Add the rice wine vinegar and blend until smooth. Cover and leave to stand for 1–2 hours before using.

2 Put the chicken, ginger and water into a saucepan, add the chopped onion and salt and bring to the boil. Simmer gently, covered, for 25 minutes. Remove the pan from the heat, keep the lid on and leave the chicken to finish cooking in the residual heat for 30 minutes.

3 Lift the chicken out of the stock and reserve both. Let the chicken cool then rub the sesame oil into the flesh.

4 Wash the rice thoroughly to remove excess starch. Heat the oil in a large saucepan and fry the garlic lightly in the oil. Add the rice, 900 ml (1½ pints) of the reserved chicken stock, the salt and pepper, then cover, bring to the boil and simmer for 20 minutes. Remove from the heat and fluff with a fork.

5 To serve, chop the chicken into pieces with a cleaver and arrange over a mound of hot rice with the cucumber, spring onions and chopped chilli, if liked. Serve the ginger pickle separately. Season the remaining stock with salt and pepper and pour into small soup bowls and serve warm topped with coriander leaves and chopped spring onions.

Serves 6

drunken chicken

qingzheng ji, china

Drunken chicken is an old Chinese dish said to date back over a thousand years to the Tang dynasty. First steamed, the chicken is then covered with Chinese wine and left to marinate to allow the flavours of the wine, ginger and Sichuan pepper to develop. Although it is simple to prepare, the chicken requires lengthy marinating for the best flavour. Serve with plain boiled rice, soy sauce and jasmine tea.

1 Rub the chicken with the salt, sugar and Sichuan pepper. Place in a container and leave to marinate overnight in the refrigerator.

2 Put the chicken into a steamer and cook for 45 minutes or until it is cooked through. To check that the chicken is cooked, make a deep cut in a leg joint; the juices must run clear.

3 Remove the chicken from the steamer and leave it to stand until it is cool enough to handle. Using a sharp knife or cleaver, chop it into bite-sized pieces and put in a container while they are still warm.

4 Mix the Chinese rice wine with the soy sauce, ginger juice and spring onions and pour over the chicken. Cover and chill in the refrigerator for 24 hours then serve cold with plain boiled rice and garnished with shredded spring onion and coriander leaves.

Serves 4

750 g (1½ lb) chicken

1 teaspoon salt

1 tablespoon caster sugar

1 teaspoon ground Sichuan pepper

300 ml (½ pint) Chinese rice wine

1 tablespoon light soy sauce

1 tablespoon Ginger Juice
(see page 8)

2 spring onions, chopped

plain boiled rice, to serve

To garnish:

1 spring onion, shredded

1 tablespoon chopped coriander leaves

braised pigeons with dried plums

hung siew ge, china

Pigeon is very popular in China, particularly in Canton. In this recipe, the pigeons are braised slowly in a red stock infused with medicinal herbs such as dang gui *(dried angelica root), which can be found in Chinese supermarkets and herbalists. In some places ginseng is also added for an extra kick.*

1 Place the pigeons in a bowl. Mix the Chinese five spice powder, ginger, garlic and star anise with the soy sauce and pour over the pigeons. Cover and leave to marinate for 1 hour.

2 Remove the pigeons from the marinade, reserving the marinade. Shake off any excess marinade and dry the pigeons with kitchen paper.

3 Heat the oil in a wok and fry the pigeons on all sides for 5–6 minutes or until brown. Remove from the oil and drain on kitchen paper.

4 Place the remaining marinade, the Chinese wine, hoisin or plum sauce, brown sugar, chicken stock, angelica, if using, and drained plums in the remaining oil in the wok or a saucepan and bring to the boil. Continue to boil for 10 minutes. Remove the star anise. Add ¼ teaspoon black pepper and mix the cornflour with a little water to make a paste and add to the sauce. Stir constantly and simmer until the sauce has thickened.

5 Add the pigeons to the sauce, cover and simmer very gently for 1 hour or until the pigeons are tender. Season to taste with salt and pepper and serve with boiled rice.

Serves 4

---

4 oven-ready pigeons

2 teaspoons Chinese five spice powder

5 cm (2 inch) piece of fresh root ginger, peeled and shredded

1 garlic clove, crushed

2 star anise

2 tablespoons dark soy sauce

4 tablespoons vegetable oil

4 tablespoons red Chinese rice wine or dry sherry

2 tablespoons hoisin or plum sauce

1 tablespoon brown sugar

450 ml (¾ pint) chicken stock or water

15 g (½ oz) dried angelica root (optional)

50 g (2 oz) dried plums, soaked in hot water for 2–3 hours

2 teaspoons cornflour

salt and pepper

boiled rice, to serve

4 duck portions

2 teaspoons Chinese five spice powder

2 lemon grass stalks, bruised

5 garlic cloves, crushed

4 red shallots, chopped

125 g (4 oz) dried shiitake mushrooms, soaked for 30 minutes

5 cm (2 inch) piece of fresh root ginger, peeled and cut into thick julienne

600 ml (1 pint) coconut water or chicken stock

25 g (1 oz) dried medlar berries or Chinese red dates

15 g (½ oz) dried black fungus (see page 8), broken into pieces

1 tablespoon fish sauce

2 teaspoons cornflour

4 spring onions, each cut into four

salt and pepper

handful of mint sprigs, to serve

aromatic braised duck

vit gung luoc, vietnam

Duck (vit) is very popular in Vietnam, where it is given an intense flavour by slow braising with a variety of oriental seeds and berries. Keep a lookout for them in Chinese supermarkets and herbalists. Stir-fried pak choi or water spinach and plain boiled rice are good accompaniments to this dish.

1 Season the duck portions with the five spice powder. Place the duck skin-side down in a very hot frying pan or casserole to brown the skin. Add the lemon grass, garlic, shallots, mushrooms and ginger to the pan then cover the duck with the coconut water or chicken stock. Cover the pan with a lid and simmer very gently for 1½ hours.

2 Remove the duck from the pan and add the medlar berries or Chinese red dates, black fungus, fish sauce and season with salt and pepper to taste. Mix the cornflour to a smooth paste with a little water and add to the pan. Stirring constantly, bring the sauce to the boil and cook until thickened. Return the duck to the pan and simmer gently for 30 minutes.

3 Add the spring onions to the sauce and serve the duck with sprigs of fresh mint.

Serves 4

tea smoked duck

jern cha yarou, china

1 tablespoon salt

1 tablespoon ground Sichuan
pepper

4 x 150 g (5 oz) duck breasts,
skinned

3 whole star anise

50 g (2 oz) rice

50 g (2 oz) Assam or China tea

50 g (2 oz) dark brown sugar

To serve:

20 ready-made Chinese pancakes

5 spring onions, shredded

10 cm (4 inch) piece of cucumber,
shredded

6–8 tablespoons plum or chilli
sauce

Home smoking can easily be done with a large wok, a trivet and a big sheet of foil. Smoking meat over tea and rice creates a lovely flavour, which permeates the meat. Thinly slice the duck while it is still warm and serve with ready-made Chinese pancakes or plain rice and plum sauce or a sweet chilli sauce.

1 Mix the salt and Sichuan pepper and rub all over the duck breasts. Set aside for 1 hour to let the flavours to develop.

2 Line a wok with a large sheet of foil, allowing plenty of overlap, and place the wok over a moderate heat. Mix together the star anise, rice, tea and sugar and add to the wok. Spread over the surface of the wok and place a trivet over the mixture. Place the duck breasts on the trivet, cover with a lid and tightly tuck in the extra foil to make a tight-fitting seal.

3 Cook over a moderate heat and when steam can be seen coming out from under the lid or foil then cook for a further 10 minutes, or 3–4 minutes longer for medium-rare meat. Remove the duck from the wok and place it in a steamer with the pancakes and steam for 5 minutes. Leave to stand for a further 3 minutes then slice thinly and serve with the pancakes, spring onions, cucumber and plum or chilli sauce.

Serves 2–3

beef cooked in vinegar

bo nhung dam, vietnam

Cook-as-you-eat dishes are very popular in Vietnam. This one is made with either the best quality beef or seafood such as prawns and squid or even clams. Traditionally the cooking liquor is brought to the table in a charcoal-fuelled steamboat accompanied by two platters with the beef and the rice papers, Vietnamese mint, coriander and purslane leaves. The dish is often served with slices of green banana or green mango but unless there is a Vietnamese or Indian store near you, these are difficult ingredients to come by.

1 Place the beef in the freezer for 1 hour to firm up; this makes it easier to slice thinly. Slice the beef and arrange on a serving plate.

2 Put the rice vinegar, water, ginger, tomatoes, lemon grass, onion, garlic and spring onions in a saucepan and bring to the boil. Boil briskly for 5 minutes. Add the salt and sugar and pour into a steamboat or fondue pot.

3 Divide the rice papers, mint, coriander and star fruit between individual serving plates. Bring the bubbling stock, the plate of beef, the rice papers and the nuoc mam dipping sauce to the table.

4 To eat, each person puts a few pieces of beef into the simmering stock and cooks it to their taste. They lift it out of the stock with chopsticks, place it on a rice paper wrapper with a few herb leaves and roll up into a cigar shape, which they dip into the nuoc mam sauce, and eat with the star fruit, if liked. The leftover broth can be drunk as a soup.

Serves 4

500 g (1 lb) beef sirloin or fillet

300 ml (½ pint) rice wine vinegar

600 ml (1 pint) water

7 cm (3 inch) piece of fresh root ginger, peeled and sliced

2 tomatoes, quartered

1 large lemon grass stalk, chopped

1 onion, halved and thickly sliced

3 garlic cloves, crushed

4 spring onions, chopped

1 teaspoon salt

1 tablespoon caster sugar

To serve:

24 prepared rice papers (see page 32)

handful of mint leaves

handful of coriander leaves

1 star fruit, thinly sliced (optional)

1 quantity Nuoc Mam Dipping Sauce (see page 94)

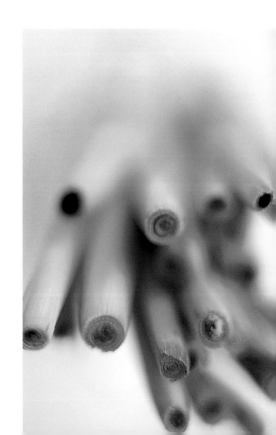

vegetables, lentils & salads

Vegetable dishes are common throughout Asia, in partcular where Buddhist beliefs include a vegetarian diet. In China the majority of dishes like Pak Choi with Garlic and Oyster Sauce (see page 117) are served as an accompanying dish. Goanese Pumpkin and Sweet Onions (see page 120) is very hot, sweet and sour; typical Goanese characteristics. In Thailand the salads (*yams*) can be vegetable based or meat based like Nua Nam Tok (see page 117), an interesting cold beef salad. Indonesia's most popular salad is Gado-gado (see page 122) a mix of tempe, tofu and vegetables in a spicy peanut sauce. Lentils are most popular in India where they are served as a major source of protein; a simple yellow split pea daal is served at most meals.

braised chive flowers
with prawns

phat phak gau choy yaang, thailand

Flowering chives (gau choy) are eaten all over South-east Asia, from China to Malaysia. They are used in China for flavouring dim sum and are also stir-fried as a vegetable. They have a strong garlic aroma and are best when very fresh. Keep them, wrapped, in the bottom of the refrigerator for up to 2 days.

1 tablespoon groundnut oil

2 garlic cloves, crushed

175 g (6 oz) flowering chives, large chives or spring onions, cut into 7 cm (3 inch) lengths

1 tablespoon fish sauce

3 tablespoons dark soy sauce

2 teaspoons caster sugar

250 g (8 oz) small raw prawns, peeled and roughly chopped

red chillies, sliced, to garnish

Thai jasmine rice, to serve (optional)

1 Heat the oil in a wok or large frying pan and add the garlic and stir-fry for 1 minute. Add the chives or spring onions, fish sauce, soy sauce and sugar and stir fry for 1 further minute.

2 Add the raw prawns to the wok and stir-fry for 3 minutes until pink and cooked through. Serve immediately, garnished with red chillies. Thai jasmine rice makes a good accompaniment.

Serves 4

mixed vegetables indian-style

sabzi, india

2 tablespoons vegetable oil

1 onion, chopped

1 garlic clove, crushed

1 teaspoon ground cumin

½ teaspoon turmeric

1 teaspoon black mustard seeds

1 teaspoon garam masala

2.5 cm (1 inch) piece of fresh root ginger, peeled and finely chopped

2 green chillies, finely chopped

125 g (4 oz) carrots, chopped

125 g (4 oz) green beans, trimmed and halved

1 drumstick vegetable (see page 6), sliced, or 1 courgette, sliced

175 g (6 oz) cauliflower, broken into florets

25 g (1 oz) fresh fenugreek leaves (methi), chopped

400 g (13 oz) can chopped tomatoes

300 ml (½ pint) vegetable stock or water

1 tablespoon Tamarind Water (see page 9)

1 tablespoon chopped coriander leaves

salt and pepper

Indian Balloon Bread (see page 141), warmed or basmati rice, to serve

This type of sabzi is cooked to accompany Indian Balloon Bread (see page 141), which are deep-fried and served as part of a breakfast. Any vegetables can be used, but drumsticks (seeng) are most often included, and potatoes (aloo) and cauliflower (gobi).

1 Heat the oil in a large frying pan or saucepan and fry the onion over a low heat for about 20 minutes or until soft, golden brown and caramelized.

2 Add the garlic and fry for 1 minute, then add the ground cumin, turmeric, black mustard seeds and garam masala. Fry for 1 further minute or until the aroma of the spices is released and the mustard seeds begin to pop.

3 Add the ginger, green chillies, carrots, beans, drumstick, cauliflower, fenugreek leaves and tomatoes and cook in the flavoured oil for 2 minutes.

4 Add the vegetable stock or water and tamarind water, bring to the boil, cover and simmer for 30 minutes or until the vegetables are tender. Season to taste and stir in the chopped coriander. Serve with warm Indian balloon bread or boiled basmati rice.

Serves 4

beef salad

nua nam tok, thailand

2 tablespoons glutinous rice

500 g (1 lb) sirloin beef

150 ml (¼ pint) water

1 lemon grass stalk, finely chopped

4 spring onions, chopped

3 tablespoons chopped mint

1 teaspoon ground chilli

2 kaffir lime leaves, shredded

2 tablespoons fish sauce

¼ teaspoon caster sugar

To serve:

baby Cos or little gem lettuce leaves

flowering chives

Salads (yams) are an important part of a Thai meal. This beef salad combines a mixture of flavours and textures: duck, squid and tuna can be prepared in the same way. To retain the full flavour and juiciness, make sure the meat is undercooked.

1 Dry-fry the rice in a heavy-based frying pan, stirring constantly for about 5 minutes or until it is golden brown.

2 Remove the rice from the heat and grind it to a fine powder in a spice grinder or use a pestle and mortar.

3 Place the beef under a preheated hot grill and cook on each side for 2 minutes. Remove from the heat, allow to stand for 10 minutes then slice thinly.

4 Bring the water to the boil in a large saucepan with the lemon grass. Remove the pan from the heat and add all the remaining ingredients, plus the beef and any cooking juices.

5 Leave the beef to cool in the liquid. Serve cold with the lettuce leaves and some flowering chives.

Serves 4

pak choi with garlic & oyster sauce

su chao qing cai, china

1 tablespoon fermented black beans

500 g (1 lb) pak choi, trimmed

3 tablespoons vegetable oil

2 garlic cloves, crushed

2 tablespoons soy sauce

3 tablespoons oyster sauce

4 tablespoons water

boiled rice, to serve

Stir-fried green vegetables with garlic and black beans are popular in China. Use pak choi, bok choi or choi sum but do not overcook them; the leaves should retain their crisp texture.

1 Rinse the black beans to get rid of any excess salt. Put them into a bowl of hot water and leave to soften for 10 minutes. Drain.

2 Roughly chop the larger pak choi leaves or quarter small pak choi.

3 Heat the oil in a wok or large frying pan, add the garlic and stir-fry for 1 minute. Add the pak choi and stir to coat in the oil.

4 Mix the soy and oyster sauces with the water and add to the wok with the black beans. Stir-fry quickly over a high heat for 1 minute and serve with plain boiled rice.

Serves 4

green papaya salad

som tam, thailand

Som tam *is found in restaurants all over Thailand and Laos. It is always made to order and will be varied according to how much chilli heat is preferred. In some parts of north-east Thailand and Laos, soft-shell crabs are added to the initial pounding. Green papaya can be found in oriental stores but otherwise use grated carrot or unripe mango.*

1 Roughly grate the papaya flesh or cut it into fine shreds.

2 Pound the garlic, chillies and cherry tomatoes to a rough purée using a large pestle and mortar.

3 Add the grated papaya, fish sauce, sugar, lime juice and dried shrimp and pound together until roughly mixed.

4 Add the chopped peanuts and coriander leaves and serve. Garnish with the extra red bird chillies and coriander leaves.

Serves 4

375 g (12 oz) green papaya, peeled

2 garlic cloves, crushed

3 red bird chillies, chopped, plus extra to garnish

4 cherry tomatoes

2 tablespoons fish sauce

2 teaspoons caster sugar

juice of 1 lime

1 tablespoon dried shrimp

3 tablespoons roasted peanuts, chopped

2 tablespoons roughly chopped coriander leaves, plus extra to garnish

minced fish salad

larb plaa, laos

Larb *is most often found in Issan, in north-east Thailand, and in Laos. In both these countries this type of local food is eaten with the fingers and not the more usual spoon and fork. It is always served cold with warm sticky rice and a few lettuce leaves for scooping it up. It can also be made with chicken, beef or pork.*

1 Roughly mince the fish and set aside.

2 Heat the oil in a wok or frying pan and fry the shallots and garlic until softened. Add the fish, galangal, fish sauce, chilli powder, sugar and lime juice and simmer for 3–4 minutes or until the fish has just cooked through. Remove from the heat and add the toasted rice, chopped mint and spring onions and mix together.

3 Serve lukewarm or cold with sticky rice and Cos lettuce leaves.

Serves 4

500 g (1 lb) haddock, catfish or cod, filleted and skinned

2 tablespoons groundnut oil or vegetable oil

2 shallots, finely chopped

1 garlic clove, crushed

2.5 cm (1 inch) piece of fresh galangal, peeled and finely chopped

2 tablespoons fish sauce

½ teaspoon chilli powder

2 teaspoons caster sugar

1 tablespoon lime juice

1 tablespoon ground toasted rice (see page 22)

1 tablespoon finely chopped mint

3 spring onions, finely chopped

To serve:

1 quantity Sticky Rice (see page 45)

Cos lettuce leaves

pumpkin & sweet onions

kaddu subzi, india

3–4 tablespoons vegetable oil

3 large onions, chopped

1 garlic clove, crushed

2 teaspoons garam masala

½ teaspoon ground cloves

750 g (1½ lb) pumpkin, peeled and roughly chopped

2 red chillies, finely chopped

4 curry leaves

200 g (7 oz) canned chopped tomatoes

300 ml (½ pint) water

2 teaspoons dark brown sugar

1 tablespoon white wine vinegar

salt and pepper

In southern Goa they cook pumpkin in this delicious sweet but chilli-hot curry. As with all Goanese cooking, vinegar is added once the curry has reduced to a thick sauce. Serve with Chicken Shakuti (see page 59) or Fish Masala with Coconut Sambal (see page 63).

1 Heat the oil in a saucepan and fry the onions for 20 minutes or until golden brown and caramelized.

2 Add the garlic, garam masala and ground cloves to the onions and cook for 1 minute, stirring constantly.

3 Add the chopped pumpkin to the pan, toss in the oil for a couple of minutes until beginning to brown. Add the chopped chillies, curry leaves, tomatoes, water and brown sugar, cover and simmer gently for 25–30 minutes or until the pumpkin is very tender.

4 Add the vinegar, season to taste with salt and pepper and serve.

Serves 4

sweet & sour aubergine

aloo baigan, india

6 tablespoons vegetable oil

4 sweet onions, chopped

2 garlic cloves, crushed

1 teaspoon garam masala

½ teaspoon turmeric

½ teaspoon chilli powder

½ teaspoon fennel seeds, crushed

750 g (1½ lb) baby aubergines, trimmed and halved

2 teaspoons brown sugar

juice of ½ lemon

5 cm (2 inch) piece of fresh root ginger, peeled and grated

2 tablespoons chopped coriander

salt and pepper

For this recipe, use either diced Mediterranean aubergines or the small Indian variety which only need to be cut in half. Keep the pan hot while browning the aubergines, otherwise they will absorb all the oil like a sponge. Cook them at a high heat and fast. The ginger and coriander are added to this balti-style dish at the end so they retain their fresh flavours.

1 Heat the oil in a saucepan, add the onions and garlic and fry gently for 15 minutes or until golden brown and caramelized.

2 Add the garam masala, turmeric, chilli powder and fennel seeds and fry for 1 minute to cook the spices. Add the aubergines and fry for 2–3 minutes, stirring constantly, to brown them on all sides.

3 Add the sugar and lemon juice, cover the pan and simmer gently for 20 minutes until the aubergines are soft and cooked through. Season well with salt and pepper then add the ginger and coriander and simmer for 5 minutes then serve.

Serves 4

morning glory vine

phak bung fai daeng, thailand

2 tablespoons vegetable oil

1 garlic clove, sliced

1 red bird chilli, chopped

500 g (1 lb) water spinach or watercress, roughly chopped

3 tablespoons light soy sauce

2 teaspoons caster sugar

1 tablespoon rice wine

1 tablespoon yellow bean paste

1 tablespoon oyster sauce

1 tablespoon fish sauce

2 tablespoons water

Phak bung fai daeng is a highlight of the Thai evening street market. The stalls that cook this speciality can be seen from far away, since all the ingredients are thrown into one enormous wok containing very hot oil. As the ingredients hit the oil they explode creating momentary flames and a lot of drama. Of course, this isn't necessary at home, but the wok does need to reach quite a heat. Morning glory vine is also known by its Chinese names of kangkung and ong choi. It is a water spinach, easily recognised by its distinctive hollow stem and triangular shaped leaves.

1 Heat the oil in a wok or large frying pan, add the sliced garlic and chilli and stir-fry for 30 seconds.

2 Add the water spinach and stir in the oil for 1–2 minutes or until it begins to wilt.

3 Mix the soy sauce, sugar, rice wine, yellow bean paste, oyster sauce, fish sauce and water together and add to the pan. Quickly stir-fry for 1 minute then serve while the spinach still has texture.

Serves 4

black lentil dal

daal makani, india

2 tablespoons ghee or butter

1 large onion, finely chopped

3 garlic cloves, crushed

7 cm (3 inch) piece of fresh root ginger, peeled and finely chopped

2 teaspoons ground coriander

1 teaspoon ground cumin

2 teaspoons garam masala

500 g (1 lb) black (*urid*) or dark brown lentils, soaked overnight

1.2 litres (2 pints) water

4 tablespoons double cream

1 tablespoon grated root ginger

1–2 tablespoons chopped coriander

salt and pepper

This black dal is a northern Indian speciality. In the foothills of the Himalayas, there is a town called Dehra Dun, where I first sampled this rich and aromatic lentil dish at a celebration supper in honour of the Dalai Lama and his Tibetan people. There, it is cooked long and slow, in little individual earthenware pots with plenty of garlic and ginger. It is a good accompaniment to Raan of Lamb (see page 97).

1 Heat the ghee or butter in a large saucepan and fry the onion for 10 minutes or until golden brown and caramelized. Add the garlic, ginger, ground coriander, cumin and garam masala and fry, stirring constantly, for 1 minute or until the aroma of the spices has been released.

2 Drain the lentils, add to the pan and coat in the ghee and spices. Add the water and bring to the boil. Reduce the heat and simmer very gently, covered, for 2–2½ hours.

3 Stir the cream into the lentils with the grated ginger and chopped coriander and season with salt and pepper to taste, replace the lid and simmer gently for a further 20 minutes.

Serves 4

spicy peanut salad

gado-gado, indonesia

175 g (6 oz) potatoes

125 g (4 oz) yard beans

2 carrots, cut into matchsticks

125 g (4 oz) white cabbage, shredded

75 g (3 oz) bean sprouts

8 cherry tomatoes, quartered

150 g (5 oz) tempe (see right), sliced and toasted

75 g (3 oz) deep-fried tofu, sliced

2 tablespoons chopped coriander

Peanut sauce:

125 g (4 oz) ground roasted peanuts

1 medium red chilli, finely chopped

1 tablespoon vegetable oil

3 shallots, finely chopped

2 garlic cloves, crushed

3 tablespoons sweet soy sauce (*ketchup manis*)

4 tablespoons water

2 teaspoons lime juice

salt and pepper

To serve:

3 hard-boiled eggs, halved

3 tablespoons deep-fried shallots (see page 8)

handful of prawn crackers (*krupuk*)

lime wedges

This large cooked salad is a great Indonesian speciality. Cooked potatoes, blanched green vegetables and slices of tempe and tofu are dressed with a sauce, similar to a peanut satay sauce. Tempe is a fermented soybean cake with a nutty flavour and firm texture. It can be found in oriental stores. However, if it proves too difficult to find, increase the amount of fried tofu. Serve the salad with Indonesian prawn crackers and add extra chilli for those who like it.

1 To make the peanut sauce, put all the ingredients in a food processor and blend until smooth or use a pestle and mortar. Put the mixture in a heavy-based saucepan and gently simmer, covered, for about 45 minutes, stirring frequently. Remove from the heat. Season to taste.

2 Boil the potatoes for 10–12 minutes until soft but still firm. Drain well, cool and slice.

3 Place the beans, carrots, cabbage and bean sprouts in a bowl, pour boiling water over them and blanch for 1 minute. Drain and refresh with cold water.

4 Arrange the blanched vegetables, the potatoes and the tomatoes on serving plates. Add the tempe, tofu, chopped coriander and hard-boiled eggs. Just before serving pour some of the warm peanut sauce over the salad. Top with crisp fried shallot and prawn crackers and serve with lime wedges.

Serves 4

seaweed salad

ao nori namasu, japan

The Japanese enthuse greatly over the properties of seaweed and sea cucumbers and recognize them as an important part of the north Asian diet. Many types of seaweed are harvested off the coasts of Asia and are now available here, either fresh or dried. Dried seaweed is most commonly available and needs to be soaked in cold water until softened. Fresh seaweed is often coated in rock salt to preserve it, and must be rinsed before use.

1 Place the seaweed in a bowl, cover with cold water and leave for 15 minutes to soften.

2 To make the dressing, mix the mirin, vinegar and dashi in a small saucepan with the sugar and heat gently until the sugar has dissolved. Remove from the heat and allow the mixture to cool.

3 When the seaweed has softened, drain it well and arrange it on individual plates. Dress with the sweet mirin dressing. Serve with wedges of lime or lemon to squeeze over the seaweed.

Serves 4

25 g (1 oz) mixed dried seaweed, such as dulse or sea lettuce

lime or lemon, to serve

Mirin dressing:

75 ml (3 fl oz) mirin

75 ml (3 fl oz) rice wine vinegar

75 ml (3 fl oz) Dashi (see page 17)

2 tablespoons caster sugar

potatoes & beans in coconut sauce

sayur-sayur, indonesia

This coconut and vegetable dish normally contains the indigenous jackfruit. Once it ripens, it becomes more like durian, another Asian fruit. At this stage both have a very strong smell and strange waxy texture which are not greatly liked by Westerners. As an alternative, this creamy curry can be cooked with yard beans, carrots, pumpkin and potatoes. Hard-boiled eggs simmered in this coconut sauce are also excellent.

1 Put the lemon grass, galangal or ginger and garlic in a saucepan with the water and coconut milk and bring to a gentle boil.

2 Add the red and green chillies, turmeric, shrimp paste and tamarind water to the coconut mixture and simmer for 5 minutes.

3 Add the potatoes and pumpkin to the coconut sauce and simmer for 15 minutes or until the potatoes are cooked but firm.

4 Add the beans, sambal ulek and lime juice and simmer for a further 5 minutes. Season to taste and add the basil leaves. Serve hot or cold with boiled rice and extra sambal ulek.

Serves 4

1 lemon grass stalk, finely chopped

5 cm (2 inch) piece of fresh galangal or root ginger, peeled and finely chopped

2 garlic cloves, crushed

150 ml (¼ pint) water

600 ml (1 pint) coconut milk

1 red chilli, finely chopped

1 green chilli, finely chopped

¼ teaspoon turmeric

½ teaspoon shrimp paste

1 tablespoon Tamarind Water (see page 9)

175 g (6 oz) potatoes, diced

125 g (4 oz) pumpkin, peeled and roughly chopped

125 g (4 oz) yard beans, cut into 5 cm (2 inch) lengths

2 teaspoons sambal ulek (see Glossary page 9), plus extra to serve

1 tablespoon lime juice

10 sweet basil leaves

salt and pepper

boiled rice, to serve

vegetable & fruit salad

rojak, indonesia

Rojak is a typical Javanese dish – part fruit salad and part vegetable. Mixed together in a bowl, it is a vibrant mix of flavours from chilli hot, brown sugar sweet, to crisp vegetable and acid fruit. It is most often eaten from hawkers' stalls, which are wheeled around the streets, with bells ringing to attract customers' attention. Once the order is placed, the hawker starts concocting the dish from his trolley of fruits and vegetables. Not for the faint hearted.

1 Place the chilli, shrimp paste, sugar, tamarind water and fish sauce in a food processor and blend to a smooth sauce, or use a pestle and mortar.

2 Mix together all the prepared vegetables and fruit and drizzle with some of the dressing. Toss lightly and serve with extra dressing if liked.

Serves 4

1 dried chilli, soaked for 30 minutes

¼ teaspoon shrimp paste (optional)

2 tablespoons dark brown sugar

6 tablespoons Tamarind Water (see page 9)

1 teaspoon fish sauce

50 g (2 oz) bean sprouts

50 g (2 oz) yard beans, cut into 2.5 cm (1 inch) lengths

1 star fruit, chopped

1 pink grapefruit, segmented and roughly chopped

2 small green mangoes, roughly grated

10 cm (4 inch) cucumber, chopped

125 g (4 oz) ripe pineapple, chopped

green beans with sesame dressing

goma-dare, japan

This is a typical Japanese salad of green beans with a traditional sesame dressing. Keep any unused dressing in an airtight jar, in the refrigerator, for up to a week. It can be used to dress spinach, sugar snap, grated carrot and daikon salads.

1 To make the dressing, toast the sesame seeds in a dry frying pan. Shake the pan regularly to brown the seeds evenly.

2 Grind the sesame seeds to a coarse paste then add the sugar, soy sauce, dashi and sake. Mix together well.

3 Heat the oil in a frying pan or wok and fry the beans and chilli for 2–3 minutes.

4 Arrange the beans on a serving plate and spoon the sesame dressing over and around them.

Serves 4

2 tablespoons vegetable oil

300 g (10 oz) green beans, trimmed and diagonally cut into strips

1 red chilli, finely chopped

Goma-dare dressing:

40 g (1½ oz) white sesame seeds

½ tablespoon caster sugar

3 tablespoons soy sauce

3 tablespoons Dashi (see page 17)

1 tablespoon sake

desserts

Asian desserts tend to be very sweet, although the sugar content can be reduced to taste, and, surprisingly, in Thailand they can be salty at the same time. At first, this is a strange taste experience, but it will grow on you. Coconut milk or freshly grated coconut flesh are used extensively for their creamy flavour. Try Bananas in Coconut Milk (see page 131) or Coconut Custard (see page 130). Indian desserts are also very sweet and rich and very delicious. Gulaab Jamuns (see page 134) are a popular feast day dish topped with gold leaf, along with the rich, Indian Pistachio and Saffron Ice Creams (see page 128). But when in season the bountiful supply of exotic fruit, such as the mighty mango, the Indonesian *pisang raja* (the king of bananas), guavas, lychees, longans and rambutans are eaten by the bag load.

125 g (4 oz) caster sugar

3 cardamom pods, bruised

900 ml (1½ pints) evaporated milk

150 ml (¼ pint) double cream

75 g (3 oz) pistachio nuts, finely chopped

20 saffron threads, soaked overnight in 4 tablespoons hot milk

edible gold or silver leaf, to decorate

indian pistachio & saffron ice creams

kulfi, india

Kulfi is Indian ice cream frozen in tall, thin tin moulds. Pistachio (pictured right) is a favourite flavour and saffron is delicious and has a dramatic colour but also try mango kulfi by mixing 150 ml (¼ pint) of mango purée into the basic mixture. Kulfi is normally made with full-fat milk, which can take about an hour to reduce to the right consistency, but by using evaporated milk the cooking time is greatly reduced and the chance of burning the milk is eliminated. Edible gold or silver leaf is a fine finishing touch and both can be found in Indian stores.

1 Put the sugar and cardamoms in a heavy-based saucepan with the evaporated milk and the cream and simmer for 10 minutes. Divide the milk mixture between 2 jugs and add pistachio nuts to one and the saffron and milk mixture to the other. Set aside to cool.

2 Pour the mixture into moulds and freeze until solid. To serve, turn out on to small dessert plates and decorate with gold or silver leaf.

Serves 6–8

coconut custard

sang khayaa maphrao, thailand

400 ml (14 fl oz) can coconut milk

125 g (4 oz) light brown sugar

seeds from 3 cardamom pods, crushed

4 eggs, beaten

25 g (1 oz) desiccated coconut, toasted

Hawkers can often be seen selling squares of this coconut custard at street corners in Thailand. It is a typical sight in Bangkok, where the custard is sometimes left plain and occasionally, strangely, covered with slowly cooked shallots, cooked until caramelized.

1 Lightly grease a 600 ml (1 pint) baking dish or tin.

2 Put the coconut milk, sugar and cardamom seeds in a saucepan and heat slowly, stirring frequently until the sugar dissolves.

3 Remove the coconut mixture from the heat, cool and stir in the beaten eggs.

4 Pour the mixture into the baking dish and stand it in a baking tin of cold water. Cook in the centre of a preheated oven, 180°C (350°F), Gas Mark 4, for 1 hour or until the centre of the pudding is firmly set.

5 Place the cooked custard under a preheated grill and cook until the top has browned slightly. Sprinkle with the toasted coconut then leave to cool slightly before chilling in the refrigerator until required.

6 To serve, cut the custard into 7 cm (3 inch) squares and place on plates lined with banana leaves.

Serves 4

tapioca and coconut soup

gula kelapa pisang sop, malaysia and laos

1.2 litres (2 pints) coconut milk

150 ml (¼ pint) water

75 g (3 oz) light brown sugar

½ teaspoon salt

50 g (2 oz) tapioca pearls

2 small bananas, roughly sliced

In Malaysia and Indonesia tapioca pearls are often used in puddings, particularly in the brightly coloured, shaved ice confections seen in the night food markets.

1 Place the coconut milk, water, sugar and salt in a saucepan. Bring to the boil, add the tapioca. Bring back to the boil, reduce the heat and simmer for 20 minutes until the tapioca has cooked through and the soup has thickened.

2 Add the bananas to the simmering soup and cook for a further 4–5 minutes. Serve in small soup bowls.

Serves 4

bananas in coconut milk

naam waan maak kuay, laos

75 g (3 oz) caster sugar

1 pandanus (screwpine) leaf
(optional)

50 ml (2 fl oz) water

400 ml (14 fl oz) coconut milk

½ teaspoon salt

6 firm bananas or 12 apple bananas

Bananas and cream are an excellent combination but in Asia the cream is in fact coconut cream or thick coconut milk. Salt and sugar are often used together in Thai and Laotian cooking and here the coconut milk is also flavoured with pandanus (screwpine) leaves or vanilla pods. Choose firm bananas, and in particular the tiny apple bananas now available in supermarkets. Do not overcook.

1 First make a syrup. Put the sugar, pandanus leaf, if using, and water into a saucepan and heat gently until the sugar has dissolved. Increase the heat and bring to the boil, then boil without stirring for 5 minutes.

2 Reduce the heat to a slow simmer and add the coconut milk and salt. Remove the pandanus leaf.

3 Cut the bananas into thick slices, add them to the coconut mixture and simmer for 5 minutes. Remove from the heat and chill until required.

Serves 4

mango & sticky rice

khao niaw ma-muang, thailand

500 g (1 lb) glutinous rice, soaked in cold water overnight

150 g (5 oz) caster sugar

1 teaspoon salt

400 ml (14 fl oz) coconut milk

2 ripe mangoes, peeled and sliced

Thai mangoes are juicy and sweet and go well with this pudding of glutinous rice and coconut milk. Great mounds of rice can be seen at roadside stalls in vast enamel bowls covered with clingfilm. A large spoonful of coconut rice is sold with half a peeled mango and a small bag of sweetened coconut milk tied up with an elastic band.

1 Drain the rice and rinse once more. Put the rice in a steamer lined with muslin, spread it out evenly and steam for 30 minutes or until soft but not overcooked.

2 Put the sugar, salt and coconut milk into a saucepan and simmer gently to dissolve the sugar.

3 Remove both the rice and coconut sauce from the heat. Put the rice into a bowl and pour half of the coconut sauce over it while both are still warm. Mix together well. Keep covered until ready to serve.

4 Serve the coconut rice in a bowl topped with the slices of mango, and the remaining coconut sauce poured over the mango.

Serves 4

semolina cake

hsanwinmakin, burma

250 g (8 oz) fine semolina flour

4 eggs

475 ml (16 fl oz) coconut milk

125 g (4 oz) caster sugar

750 ml (1¼ pints) water

3 tablespoons vegetable oil

75 g (3 oz) sultanas

50 g (2 oz) flaked almonds

50 g (2 oz) white sesame or poppy seeds

50 g (2 oz) butter, melted

edible gold leaf, to decorate

These diamonds of Burmese semolina cake are more like a sweetmeat than a conventional cake or pudding. Arrange them on a small plate and serve with coffee or tea at the end of a rich meal.

1 Heat a large heavy-based saucepan and add the semolina flour. Toast thoroughly, stirring constantly. Beat the eggs with the coconut milk and sugar and add to the flour with the water. Set aside for 30 minutes.

2 Heat the oil in a pan, add the semolina paste and cook over a moderate heat, stirring constantly, for about 15 minutes or until it becomes thick and heavy.

3 Mix the sultanas and almonds into the semolina and spread in a 25 cm (10 inch) square cake tin. Smooth the surface then sprinkle with the sesame seeds.

4 Drizzle the melted butter all over the surface of the semolina and put it under a preheated grill until it becomes a light golden brown.

5 Place the tin in the centre of a preheated oven, 200°C (400°F), Gas Mark 6, for about 20 minutes. Remove from the oven and leave to cool. Cut into diamond shapes and decorate with gold leaf.

Serves 8–10

malaysian pancakes

murtabak, malaysia

500 g (1 lb) plain flour

3 tablespoons vegetable oil

250 ml (8 fl oz) milk

125 ml (4 fl oz) water

6 eggs

4 tablespoons melted ghee or
vegetable oil

To serve:

150 ml (¼ pint) condensed milk

6 tablespoons chocolate sauce

lemon wedges

Malaysian night-time markets always have a murtabak stand turning out a selection of these stuffed Muslim pancakes, from curried chicken and other savoury fillings to sweet versions drizzled with condensed milk. These are square, filled pancakes made with a thin sheet of dough which is stretched to shape, like an Italian making a pizza, by throwing in the air and catching the dough. The murtabak stalls in Kota Baru, in eastern Malaysia, are some of the most popular and always attract a young crowd who eat first the savoury version and then the sweet.

1 Sift the flour into a bowl and add the oil, milk, water and 2 beaten eggs and mix to a soft dough. Turn out the dough on to a floured surface and knead for 10 minutes until smooth and elastic. Cover with clingfilm and leave to rest in a cool place for 30 minutes.

2 Divide the dough into 10 and roll out each piece to a very thin, large rectangle.

3 Beat the remaining eggs and brush the surface of the pieces of dough with plenty of egg, then fold in the two shortest sides to make an envelope.

4 Heat a cast-iron frying pan or skillet with a little ghee or vegetable oil, add 1 pancake at a time and cook for 4 minutes, turning regularly and drizzling with melted ghee in between. Fold the pancake in half, press down and cook for a further 2 minutes on either side.

5 Remove the pancake from the pan and drizzle with plenty of condensed milk and chocolate sauce. Roll up tightly into a cigar shape and serve wrapped in a napkin with a wedge of lemon.

Makes 10

rosewater milk balls

gulaab jamuns, india

500 g (1 lb) caster sugar

600 ml (1 pint) water

juice of ¼ lemon

3 cardamoms, bruised

1 tablespoon rosewater

150 g (5 oz) dried milk powder

50 g (2 oz) self-raising flour

2 teaspoon baking powder

5–6 tablespoons cold water

14 pistachio nuts, shelled

oil, for deep-frying

chopped pistachio nuts, to serve

edible gold leaf, to decorate

Rosewater (gulaab) milk balls are first deep-fried and then poached in a rosewater sugar syrup. Light and delicately flavoured they are a fragrant way to end an Indian meal. When first added to the oil they will sink to the bottom of the pan. If the temperature is correct, within a minute they will rise to the surface. Do not fry them too quickly or they will not cook through.

1 First make the sugar syrup. Put the sugar and water into a saucepan and heat until the sugar dissolves. Add the lemon juice and cardamoms and boil to a thick syrup. Remove from the heat and set aside half of the syrup, leave to cool, then add the rosewater. Return the remaining syrup to the heat and simmer gently.

2 Sieve the milk powder, self-raising flour and baking powder together. Add some of the water a teaspoon at a time to make a soft dough and knead lightly on a floured surface for 5 minutes. Cover the dough with clingfilm and leave for 30 minutes.

3 Divide the mixture into 14 balls and stuff each ball with a pistachio. Heat the oil in a deep-fat fryer until a cube of bread is golden brown in 4 minutes. Add 4 balls to the oil and fry slowly, turning occasionally, until they are evenly reddish brown in colour.

4 Remove the cooked balls with a slotted spoon and immediately place them in the pan with the sugar syrup. Simmer gently for 5 minutes. Repeat with the remaining milk balls.

5 Remove the cooked milk balls from the simmering sugar syrup and place in the chilling sugar syrup. Leave the milk balls in the syrup, in the refrigerator, for at least 1 hour before serving. Serve sprinkled with pistachio nuts and decorated with gold leaf.

Serves 4

fried bananas

pisang goreng, indonesia

150 g (5 oz) self-raising flour

1 tablespoon tapioca or plain flour

200 g (7 oz) rice flour

1 teaspoon finely grated lime rind

2 teaspoons caster sugar

400 ml (14 fl oz) cold water

8–10 bananas, sliced lengthways

oil, for deep-frying

icing sugar, for dusting

Pisang Goreng are a favourite roadside snack which are sold by the bag, fresh out of the hot oil. Pisang Moleng are similar but these are wrapped in very thin puff pastry and then fried. Pisang Goreng are best made with firm bananas but an apple banana or plantain will do. Serve with Spiced Indonesian Tea (see page 142).

1 Sift the self-raising flour, tapioca and rice flour into a bowl and stir in the grated lime rind and sugar. Slowly add the water and beat to a smooth batter.

2 Heat the oil in a deep-fryer or wok until hot enough to brown a cube of bread in 3–4 minutes. Dip the pieces of banana into the batter and then straight into the hot oil. Deep-fry about 6 pieces of banana at a time, turning them once. When the bananas are crisp and golden brown, remove them with a slotted spoon and drain on kitchen paper.

3 To serve, sprinkle with icing sugar and eat while still warm.

Serves 4–6

black rice pudding

pulit hitam, indonesia

Pulit Hitam *(black rice)* is a popular Indonesian pudding, which is also eaten at breakfast time. Creamy and dense, it is best eaten with fresh fruit such as mango, pineapple or lychees. It looks similar to wild rice and can be found in Indian and Philippino stores.

1 Wash the rice in several changes of water then place it in a large saucepan with the measured water and bring to the boil. Cover and cook at a fast simmer for about 1 hour. Add the sugar and vanilla pod and simmer for a further 20 minutes or until the rice is tender and cooked through.

2 Stir the 150 ml (¼ pint) coconut milk and the salt into the rice. Serve the rice pudding topped with shavings of fresh coconut and drizzled with the remaining coconut milk.

Serves 4–6

250 g (8 oz) black glutinous rice

2 litres (3½ pints) water

250 g (8 oz) light brown sugar

1 vanilla pod

150 ml (¼ pint) coconut milk, plus 4 tablespoons

½ teaspoon salt

50 g (2 oz) fresh coconut shavings

vermicelli & coconut soup

sevian kheer, burma

This creamy soup is made with roasted or toasted vermicelli which can be bought ready-made from Asian stores. Alternatively it needs to be fried in ghee (clarified butter). A northern Indian or Burmese dish, it is very rich and only a small amount is required for each serving.

1 Melt the ghee, add the vermicelli and fry, stirring constantly, until it is golden brown on all sides.

2 Soak the saffron threads in 4 tablespoons of the warm milk for at least 20 minutes.

3 Bring the remaining milk to the boil, and add the vermicelli, crushed cardamom pods and soaked saffron. Simmer gently, stirring occasionally, for about 10 minutes or until the vermicelli is cooked and the liquid has reduced and thickened.

4 Add the sugar, toasted almonds and raisins and simmer for 5 minutes.

5 Serve in soup bowls and eat with a soup spoon.

Serves 4

125 g (4 oz) ghee

50 g (2 oz) vermicelli, cut into 5 cm (2 inch) lengths

15 saffron threads

1.5 litres (2½ pints) warm milk or coconut milk

10 cardamom pods, crushed

50 g (2 oz) caster sugar

50 g (2 oz) flaked almonds, toasted

75 g (3 oz) raisins

accompaniments & drinks

In Asian cooking it is all the little extras that are eaten on an everyday basis that complete the dish. The Japanese wasabi paste and pickled ginger that accompany sushi, the Burmese balachaung condiment, the jars of ground roasted peanuts that are on every table alongside dried chilli flakes, sugar and fish sauce. Fish sauce is used in Thai cooking as often as we add salt and pepper. Tamarind Chutney (see page 140) is very popular in south India and is served with Indian breads. When it gets too hot, ice cold Lassi (see page 142) is the perfect choice.

fenugreek paratha with tamarind chutney

methi paratha, india

500 g (1 lb) strong wholemeal plain flour

150 g (5 oz) ghee or butter, melted

150 ml (¼ pint) milk

2 tablespoons water

1 egg, beaten

125 g (4 oz) fenugreek leaves or spinach, chopped

1 tablespoon chopped coriander leaves

Tamarind chutney:

½ teaspoon chilli powder

2 teaspoons garam masala

1 onion, chopped

½ teaspoon salt

¼ teaspoon black pepper

150 g (5 oz) tamarind pulp

300 ml (½ pint) water

125 g (4 oz) dark brown sugar

Paratha can be served throughout the day from breakfast, with honey and yogurt, to dinnertime when it is served plain with a distinctive curry or as here stuffed with fenugreek. Mrs George, one of the renowned cooks from Wellington Indian Army Staff College in Tamil Nadu, made these for our picnic. Her tamarind chutney is the ideal accompaniment to parathas and samosas.

1 To make the tamarind chutney, dry-fry the chilli and garam masala in a heavy-based saucepan. Add all the remaining chutney ingredients and heat gently to dissolve the sugar and the tamarind pulp. Bring to the boil and boil for 5 minutes. Remove the pan from the heat. Leave the chutney to cool then strain it into a sterilized jar.

2 Sift the flour into a bowl and rub in 50 g (2 oz) of the ghee or butter. Combine the milk, water and egg and add to the flour with the fenugreek and coriander. Mix together until resembling a dough. Turn out the dough on to a floured surface and knead for 10 minutes or until the mixture becomes smooth and elastic. Cover with clingfilm and leave to rest for 1 hour.

3 Divide the mixture into 12 pieces and work with one at a time, keeping the rest covered with a damp tea towel to prevent the dough from drying out.

4 Melt the remaining ghee or butter. Roll each piece of dough into a long thin sausage then coil it into a round. Flatten to a 12 cm (5 in) round with the palm of the hand or a rolling pin and sprinkle with the melted ghee or butter.

5 Heat a heavy-based frying pan and cook each paratha for 3–4 minutes on each side or until golden brown and crisp. Remove and repeat with the remaining dough.

Makes 12

pickled cucumber

ajad, thailand

125 g (4 oz) cucumber, diced

1 shallot, finely sliced

1 small carrot, diced

1 red bird chilli, finely sliced

2 teaspoons caster sugar

4 tablespoons water

150 ml (¼ pint) rice wine vinegar

¼ teaspoon salt

Pickled cucumber is often served with Satay (see page 31) along with Pressed Rice. It can be made in advance and kept in the refrigerator in a screw-top jar for 2–3 days.

1 Place the cucumber, shallot, carrot and chilli in a sterilized jam jar.

2 Put the sugar and water into a saucepan and heat gently, stirring constantly, until the sugar has dissolved. Remove from the heat and leave to cool.

3 Add the vinegar and salt to the sugar syrup and pour over the vegetables. Cover and leave to stand for 1 hour before using.

Makes 300 ml (½ pint)

sweet chilli sauce

siracha, thailand

15 medium chillies

250 g (8 oz) granulated sugar

150 ml (¼ pint) rice wine vinegar

150 ml (¼ pint) water

½ teaspoon salt

¼ teaspoon pepper

juice of 1 lemon

This sweet chilli sauce is a good dipping sauce for Thai Barbecued Chicken (see page 91), Thai Fish Cakes (see page 27) or deep-fried chicken or fish. Although traditionally Thai, it could quite easily be served with Indian Pakoras (see page 26). It will keep for up to 1 month in the refrigerator.

1 Wearing a pair of plastic gloves, remove the seeds from the chillies and finely chop the flesh. Place the chillies in a saucepan with the sugar, rice vinegar and water. Heat gently to dissolve the sugar then increase the heat and simmer briskly for 20–25 minutes or until the liquid has reduced to a syrup.

2 Remove the pan from the heat and leave to cool. Add the salt, pepper and lemon juice. Pour the sauce into a sterilized glass jar or bottle and keep in the refrigerator until required.

Makes 300 ml (½ pint)

indian balloon breads

puri, india

250 g (8 oz) strong wholemeal plain flour

½ teaspoon salt

25 g (1 oz) ghee or butter

175 ml (6 fl oz) warm water

2 teaspoons vegetable oil

groundnut oil, for deep-frying

Puri and Sabzi (see page 116) are the way to start the Indian day. The potato-based vegetable curry is scooped up and eaten with the deep-fried bread. Puris are traditionally deep-fried in ghee, although for a healthier alternative these are cooked in groundnut oil.

1 Sift the flour into a bowl with the salt. Rub the ghee or butter into the flour then mix in the water and vegetable oil to make a dough.

2 Turn the dough out on to a floured surface and knead for 10 minutes or until it is soft and elastic. Cover with oiled clingfilm and leave to rest for 1 hour.

3 Lightly knead the dough once more then divide the dough into 12 equal-sized balls. Roll each one out to a 12 cm (5 inch) round.

4 Heat the groundnut oil in a deep-fryer or wok until a cube of bread browns in 2 minutes. Add a round of dough to the hot oil. The dough should sink to the bottom of the oil and almost immediately rise to the top and start to puff up. Once it has puffed, turn it over and cook for 1 further minute on the second side or until it is golden brown all over.

5 Remove with a slotted spoon and drain on kitchen paper for 30 seconds. Serve the puris immediately before they begin to deflate.

Makes 12

saffron lassi

lassi, india

3 tablespoons hot milk

15 saffron threads

½ teaspoon cumin seeds

300 ml (½ pint) thick natural yogurt

¼ teaspoon salt

1 teaspoon caster sugar

300 ml (½ pint) water, chilled

cracked ice cubes, to serve

A golden saffron lassi is quite something. The first one I ever tried was in Rajasthan. It was very cooling, and its intense saffron flavour was quite delicious. Lassi can be served sweet or salty, flavoured with rosewater or puréed fruit like mango; for a mango lassi, substitute 1 large puréed mango for the saffron milk in this recipe. These are most refreshing drinks when the heat of the summer becomes too strong.

1 Pour the milk over the saffron and set aside for 1–2 hours to soak.

2 Heat a frying pan until hot then add the cumin seeds and toast for 1–2 minutes or until you can smell the cumin. Remove from the heat and leave to cool.

3 Put the yogurt, salt, sugar and water into a food processor and blend for 30 seconds. Add the toasted cumin and blend for 1 minute. Add the soaked saffron and liquid to the yogurt mixture and blend briefly until combined.

4 Fill a jug with cracked ice cubes, pour the lassi over the ice and serve.

Serves 4

spiced indonesian tea

bandrek, indonesia

2 dried red bird chillies

5 cm (2 inch) piece of fresh root ginger, peeled and roughly chopped

5 whole cloves

1 small cinnamon stick

½ teaspoon black peppercorns

3 cardamom pods, bruised

600 ml (1 pint) tea

1–2 tablespoons brown sugar

On Pulah Weh, the most northern island of Sumatra, they brew a fine Indonesian bitter tea, tea pahit or bandrek, as it is more commonly known. It is regularly drunk by men, women and children with the local fried bananas, Pisang Goreng (see page 136). Spiced tea is a thirst-quenching drink when the summer is hot, and doubles as a warming brew during the winter.

1 Place the chillies, ginger, cloves, cinnamon, peppercorns, cardamom pods and tea into a saucepan, bring to the boil, cover and simmer for 10 minutes.

2 Remove from the heat, strain into another saucepan and return to the heat with the sugar and heat gently until the sugar has dissolved. Serve black.

Serves 4